HOW TO ENGINEER A $30M EXIT

GRAHAM MORGAN

HOW TO ENGINEER
A $30M EXIT

A guide on how to maximise the
value of your business when selling it

PROLOGUE

'It is not the critic who counts; not the man who points out how the strong man stumbles or where the doer of deeds could have done better. The credit belongs to the man who is actually in the arena, whose face is marred by dust and sweat and blood, who strives valiantly, who errs and comes up short again and again, because there is no effort without error or shortcoming, but who knows the great enthusiasms, the great devotions, who spends himself in a worthy cause; who, at the best, knows, in the end, the triumph of high achievement, and who, at the worst, if he fails, at least he fails while daring greatly, so that his place shall never be with those cold and timid souls who knew neither victory nor defeat.'

Theodore Roosevelt
Speech at the Sorbonne, Paris, April 23, 1910

ACKNOWLEDGEMENTS

You. The business owner whose 'whose face is marred by dust and sweat ... '

You are the one in the arena, the one who turns up every day, scared of what lies ahead, but you show up anyway and give it your best shot. You are the one this book is dedicated to, no matter what type or size of business you own. This book is for you, as in my view, you are brave, very brave.

I would like to thank all those who made writing this book possible, either because they support me in my work and life or because they have trusted me with one of their most valuable assets, their business. Thank you for your support, care, trust and opportunity.

To those who helped me review and edit, gave creative counsel and most of all encouraged and pushed me to complete this book and finally let it go! Thank you for your patience and care, you know who you are.

Finally, I will just mention two wonderful people who are always with me in spirit, every day and at every challenging moment – 'Shaw' and 'Morgan', thank you for your guidance and counsel and for giving me the strength and courage to go on when all looks dark and I have difficult decisions to make. And to my rock, 'Tryfan'.

Thank you all.

First published in 2024 by Graham Morgan

A catalogue entry for this book is available from the National Library of Australia.

ISBN: 978-1-922764-35-5

Printed in Australia by Pegasus
Book production and text design by Publish Central

The paper this book is printed on is certified as environmentally friendly.

Disclaimer

CONTENTS

INTRODUCTION

Once again, a sad but familiar scene. I was buying a business on behalf of a client, sitting across the negotiating table from the business owner (and his representative), and I was not going to pay them what it was worth. This wasn't because I was mean or had some secret advantage. I wasn't even a better negotiator than them. Quite simply, they had not maximised the value of their business, nor had they fully prepared their business for sale. Therefore, I would buy the business for less than its full potential.

If the owner had prepared earlier, understood what drives value through a 'buyer's eyes', took the actions required and been better represented, they could have achieved an additional $2M on the sale price. What made it worse was that I got to know the seller well through the process. I knew he needed every dollar he could get and would have to sell his family home, and that once all the outstanding debts and taxes were taken out of the sale's proceeds, he would have very little left over for himself and no income to support a significant mortgage. This was not a good result for him. In addition, because the business structure and documentation had not been adequately prepared, the whole process was difficult and time-consuming, putting additional stress and pressure on him and his wife at an already challenging time.

It was at that point that I decided to switch from buying businesses for large corporates (and making them even more financially successful) to focusing my attention on working with business owners – who had spent a lifetime's work building and running a business – and getting them the maximum price when it comes time to sell. Why should they not collect its true worth after years of hard work? It just seemed so wrong to me if they didn't. In addition, selling a business can be very stressful for all parties involved, particularly the owner. By its very nature, selling a business is intrusive and a very personal and emotional time for an owner, particularly if they have long-serving and loyal employees. Hence, I also decided to lessen the burden on the owner, keep them 'safe and sane' and give them the best chance of a life-changing payout from selling their business. This determination to maximise the value in a business and release that value in the sale while protecting the owner drove me to set up Morgan Shaw Advisory (MSA). I had not seen an advisory business focus on this 'value driver' aspect, with exceptional transactional capability and the personal element of protecting a business owner's mental health. This became my personal mission then and still is today. Having now worked with many private business owners (and being one myself), I understand just how demanding and exhausting running a business can be. A big part of them wanting to sell is simply to be released from the burden of this enormous responsibility.

Selling a business is hard. While there are over 2 million businesses in Australia, less than 1000 are sold each year. Realising its maximum value is even more challenging. Just like death and taxes, every business owner has to face the fact that one day, they will have to deal with what happens after they retire and/or die. Why is it that the transaction of selling a business, probably the most significant financial event a person can experience, does not deliver the maximum value it can? What is it that a business owner needs to do to maximise the sale of their business? Through over 50 sale and acquisition transactions that I have personally managed, I have learnt what works and what doesn't, seen some great practices and some pretty awful ones. So, I have pulled together what I believe needs to be addressed to achieve the best result an owner can. I will also share an overview of the methodology I use with my clients.

There are many reasons why a business may be 'under-prepared' for sale. Business owners are good at whatever has made their business successful, which is what they focus on. Most will have spent years building a business to give them and their customers what they want. They will probably have spent little or no time building it, thinking, 'Is this going to add value when I come to sell?'. Most will have never sold a business before or are unlikely to do so again, so they have little knowledge or expertise in managing the numerous aspects of the process of selling a business. A key issue is that people start preparing too late and do not take advice and action early enough. If a business owner leaves preparing their business for sale until they enter the selling process, it is already too late. They will almost certainly not get its true value, and the process will be more stressful than if they had started working on it 12 months earlier, delivered a value enhancement strategy and had expert guidance.

This book is not a 'How to sell your business' book; plenty of those have been written, and many will give you a good, simple step-by-step process. If you just want to sell a business, this book will take you through a typical sales process, but it has not been written for that purpose. It has been written for business owners who want to maximise their business's value *before* they enter a sales process, for those who are prepared to put in the additional effort and resources required to achieve top price for their business. Smart negotiation can only achieve so much. To maximise the amount someone will pay for your business, you must first maximise its value. I have combined my experience creating long-lasting value enhancement strategies and what I have learnt in buying and selling businesses. I have aligned this with my experience running both large and small businesses to create a unique model for each client to maximise their worth. I have had unique experiences, and my clients have unique businesses. We can create something special by combining that shared knowledge and experience. I have created my own model, the six-stage EBITDA+™ SIX STEPS TO SUCCESS, which will show what is involved in creating the additional value a buyer is prepared to pay for through to post-deal. However, what is required is more than just a smart process, and I hope that as this book unfolds, that additional ingredient will present itself to you.

I truly hope this book encourages you to be more proactive, take early action and get what you deserve from a lifetime's hard work and achievement. You always need to be 'game ready'.

SECTION 1

WHY IS IT SO HARD?

CHAPTER 1

THE AUSTRALIAN BUSINESS MARKET

According to the Australian Bureau of Statistics (as of 30 June 2022), there were more than 2.5 million actively trading businesses in Australia, and the structure of them is as follows:

- 1,550,151 of them have 0 employees. They are, in effect, single contractors who earn a living but are not employed by someone else.
- 728,759 have 1–4 employees.
- 227,102 have 5–19 employees.
- 59,355 have 20–199 employees.
- 4800 have 200+ employees.

The first thing that strikes you about these statistics is just how many businesses in Australia are really small. Small businesses are very challenging to sell and, in many cases, 'unsaleable' just due to their size. This would certainly apply to the 1.5 million businesses that have zero employees. There is little prospect of these businesses being sold unless they have some unique intellectual property (IP) that is fully licensed and protected (and, as importantly, transferrable). Those with one to four employees can be sold; however, it is still very challenging and would need some special IP or be sold to a competitor looking to grow, move premises, etc.

To describe the market for selling businesses in Australia, I will exclude those with less than five employees. This leaves us with a more probable market pool of around 290,000, not the 2.5 million registered businesses. With only about 1000 Australian businesses selling every year, that equates to 0.44% of those businesses with five or more employees. So, with what would appear to be a very low success rate, what are the market dynamics that an owner must consider when preparing to sell their business?

There are several factors why the Australian market is particularly unique/difficult:

- **The limited number of international buyers due to the geographical location of Australia.** Given Australia's distance from the rest of the world, this eliminates many potential acquirers who otherwise may be interested. As geographical synergies are likely to be non-existent, they will have concerns regarding the management of their acquisition from afar. This certainly applies to potential buyers in regions such as the USA and Europe.

- **Limited domestic buyers due to the size of Australia.** Given the significant size of Australia's land mass and the concentration of people/businesses in a relatively small number of locations, this limits who would be interested in buying companies interstate. As you will have seen from the size profile of businesses, the vast majority are small. While a number of them may be interested in acquiring other companies, it is unlikely that a small business will acquire a business in another state.

· **The proportion of small businesses.** A small business is much riskier for a buyer than a larger business as less tangible assets are being acquired, and any loss of revenue or key employees will have a much bigger impact. From a buyer's viewpoint, if a business only has a small number of employees and does not own many assets, what are they buying, and how do they retain it after acquiring it?

· **Market size.** The overall size of the market is small. As shown in the business profile, the market size is only 290,000 (and that is if you include businesses with five employees).

More positive factors include:

· **The proximity to Asia**, particularly for those industries/ companies that supply into that market. This attracts two different sets of countries:

  – Asia. There are many reasons why it makes good commercial sense for Asian companies to buy Australian businesses. For example, Asian businesses that want Australian goods supplied to their domestic market will already have distribution channels and retail outlets. They can immediately gain a significant uplift from a business that could supply into Asia but hasn't. In addition, Asian businesses looking to extend their capability in their supply chain will acquire complementary businesses, especially those that already source from Asia.

- Other countries that want to break into Asia. Australia is a great location to launch into Asia for companies that reside in areas such as North America and Europe.
- **The lifestyle.** Australia is a beautiful country with a high standard of living, good schooling and welfare, and it is relatively safe. For a business that is well run and can demonstrate that it can continue to be a successful business for a new owner, there will be a pool of potential investors across the world looking to buy a business in Australia as both an entry point (it will help with visa requirements, etc.) and a source of income as soon as they arrive. This is particularly attractive to Asian countries and those that have made their wealth across the rest of the world. This will be a growing opportunity as the 'middle class' grows in countries such as China and India.

In terms of the main type of buyers (or representatives of buyers) in the Australian business market, they can be broadly categorised as below:

- **Private equity (PE)** – PE firms typically use a combination of their funds (including those of their investors) and debt to buy businesses to grow the value of their investment significantly before selling. They will usually have an industry sector strategy, i.e. they have decided to invest in a particular industry, identify target companies to buy and then acquire several of them. They then seek to drive synergies and take back-office costs out of those businesses to make them both larger and more profitable. They are highly resourced, informed, professional buyers and can be a good purchaser for a business. They typically require the owner to remain in the business for a reasonable period or even through to their exit, which can be years away. A note of caution: they are sophisticated buyers and will look to buy as low as they can and can be demanding of a seller post-sale. They will almost certainly demand significant presence and power on the Board. You would be well advised to seek professional support before engaging with them.

- **Competitors** – A well-known business strategy for companies is to eliminate (by out-competing) or acquire competitors within their business sector. This is an adopted approach by companies in many sectors in all stages of growth or decline. They may be very experienced buyers and even have an in-house team, or it may be the first time they have acquired a business. They will be looking for immediate and obvious synergies.

- **Suppliers** – Another strong growth strategy is for a business to buy companies up and down its own supply chain. This can provide numerous benefits for the acquirer and, if done well, creates an entirely new organisation that dominates its industry sector. It is more complicated, and the immediate synergy benefits may not be as obvious. Still, if the acquirer has done their research correctly and has a clear vision of what they are building, they can be a very exciting buyer of your business, particularly for your employees and customers.

- **Corporate advisor** – Yes, we also sit on the other side of the table. Any of the other potential channels can engage a corporate advisor to do their buying for them. This can be very effective for a buyer, as it stops their management team from being distracted by potential acquisitions. It is a function best suited to outsource to a professional. As with PE companies, you should engage with a professional advisor if a professional corporate advisor represents your acquirer.

- **Family offices** – These are typically intelligent, savvy business people, passionate about seeing their investments grow and do not want to sit back. They have a good eye for business, and while they may not demand as much due diligence as some acquirers, they know what they are doing and will have worked out where the future value lies for them. They can be good acquirers in many other ways post-sale, particularly if you want to stay on and have a role in the business after you have sold. Family offices often have in-house professional teams to manage an effective and solid process. They are usually well-funded and have the capital readily available.

- **Big-tier consulting firms** – As with corporate advisors, larger consulting firms can also acquire for their larger clients. They may not run the whole process but will be engaged in certain aspects such as financial or legal due diligence, and strategic review of the sector, your business and the competitors to predict likely future value-adding opportunities. They are highly capable with significant resources, so you must again ensure that you have a strong (and equally capable) advisor in your corner with sufficient resources to match the consulting firm.

- **Private companies** – There may be several reasons a random private company would want to acquire a business outside its normal sphere. It could be that the core business is generating excess profits. Rather than leave the cash in the bank, they want to put the money to use in another business and have decided to invest it outside of their sector for whatever reason. It could be that your sector is predicted to be safe or growing, and theirs could be threatened or expected to go into decline. They may have bought several businesses, or this could be their first one. They may do all the work themselves or engage a professional.

- **Public companies** – Large public companies nearly always have an inorganic growth strategy, i.e. part of their growth strategy is to acquire other companies. Often, they will have a team in place or nominate a senior executive (e.g. the CFO) to lead the process supported by external professionals. You can expect high-level knowledge of your business or sector, as there will usually be a strategic reason for their interest in it. They will be searching for companies to buy after having completed a long-term strategic review that identified the sector you operate in is one in which they want to invest. You will be one of several businesses that they may consider. There can be several post-sale benefits, including the security of employees working for a publicly listed company. Suppose the owner wants to stay on in a role post-sale. In that case, they can quite often launch a new career with the security of having banked the proceeds from selling their business while pulling a salary.

- **Entrepreneurs/private investors** – These can come from anywhere. Entrepreneurs and private investors who are serial acquirers will likely have a process and methodology. Still, some may see a business they like, see the potential for them to add value and decide to acquire it. They can be chaotic and less secure than other potential acquirers. However, they can be an exciting acquirer with careful research and a professional process run from the seller's end.

CHAPTER 2
HOW DO PEOPLE EXIT
THEIR BUSINESSES?

When selling a business, the first consideration is: are you a proactive or a reactive seller? In other words, did you knock on someone's door and ask if they wanted to buy your business, or did they knock on yours? This can significantly affect how you approach a prospective buyer or respond to an enquiry from an interested party. In either event, how you manage those early, critical discussions may significantly impact the final price. To expand on this further, it is very flattering when someone wants to buy your business, and some businesses do get sold this way, but how do you manage the transaction/process to ensure you are getting the top price? What if they offer you a price that seems OK? I worked with a client that had been 'long-term courted' by an overseas buyer. While their initial offer seemed fair (and more than the owners had set as their minimum), by running a professional sales process and taking control, we got an additional 40% more than the initial 'fair' offer from the same buyer! To put that into personal terms, it set up the seller's grandchildren, not just their children, for life. In any event, if a prospective buyer approaches you and you believe you can manage it yourself, there are several reasons why you could benefit from professional advice at an early stage. Additionally, under no circumstances should a business owner provide confidential or commercial information to a potential acquirer without seeking professional advice unless they fully understand all aspects of a sales process. Another point to consider if someone approaches you is that a choice of one is not a choice. It is significantly limiting only to consider selling to one party from both a value and risk point of view.

An added complexity is the stage of business cycle maturity your business is in and the sector in which you operate. If your business is in a high growth phase and an attractive market sector, how you manage a sale will be very different from an established business with many physical assets in a less attractive, traditional industry. For example, take two separate businesses I bought for the same client. One was a traditional manufacturing business in a declining industry with old and tired equipment; the other was in the marketing services sector, delivering cloud-based automation solutions in a highly charged growth sector. While the manufacturing business had higher revenue and profits (and more tangible assets), my client was prepared to pay more for the marketing services business due to future growth opportunities and being in a high-performing sector that attracted higher valuations. In such cases, while the manufacturing business would usually be valued using the Earnings Before Interest, Taxes, Depreciation & Amortisation (EBITDA) multiple method, the marketing services business may be valued on a multiple of revenue. It's a similar maths equation: one uses a form of profit, and the other uses revenue.

Before we review the various channels you could choose to sell your business, let's have a high-level look at the two main types of sales structure:

1. **Asset purchase.** An asset purchase is the simpler of the two structures. In effect, what you are selling are selected assets of your business, not the shares of the business. This means that you (and not the buyer) remain responsible post-sale for the company, including any misdemeanours, taxes owing, payments to suppliers and all liabilities up to completion, including employees' superannuation, etc. As you are not selling the legal entity, there is much less legal due diligence required for the buyer to complete. Because of this simpler structure, the time taken to conduct due diligence and prepare the legals is significantly reduced, so a much swifter sales process can occur. Note that with an asset purchase, employment is not automatically transferred, and it is a vital aspect of the negotiations that needs to happen as part of the Non-Binding Indicative Offer (NBIO). The buyer must offer employment to whichever employees they wish to keep in their company if they want to employ them. If the buyer does not offer them similar roles, pay, workplace location, etc., the employees can claim redundancy from the seller of the business. Also, suppose the buyer does not offer them employment in the new entity. In that case, they are entitled to claim redundancy from the seller. Communication of the offer of employment with employees and securing those positions need careful planning and an effective process to ensure it is handled well and a positive experience for employees. The responsibility lies with the seller – morally, legally and financially – you must get good advice and

ensure you understand what is required before you speak to any employees.

2. **Share purchase.** A share purchase is exactly what it sounds like. You are selling all the shares of the business and everything that goes with it, including its history. A buyer acquiring another business's shares must complete detailed legal, financial and tax due diligence. One of the other differences is that the buyer will automatically be the employer of all staff. The employees do not have a choice whether to transfer over as the legal entity has not changed, just the owners of that entity. This also means if the buyer does not require all the staff, the responsibility for dealing with redundancies, etc., lies with the buyer.

When you are considering which of the two sale structures to adopt (bearing in mind your buyer may also have their own preference), you should seek professional tax advice as it can significantly affect the tax you pay based on the structure, size of the sale and your own personal circumstances. There is no point in maximising the amount a buyer will pay for your business if you trip up and sell it through the wrong process/structure. This is a highly specialised area, and I would encourage you to get a specialist tax accountant to advise you at the earliest stage.

There are several channels to sell a business, the main ones being:

A. Corporate advisor
B. Global banking and financial services firms
C. Big-tier consultancy firms
D. Business broker
E. Accountant or lawyer

F.   Online agencies

G.   Do-it-yourself (DIY).

As you can see, there are several options available for a business owner to sell their business, and I have put them into two groups, dependent on the type of services (strategic or transaction) they provide.

1. Strategic services

These providers offer strategic services in addition to the basic transaction process, albeit each provider's interpretation and what they offer will differ from each other. If you decide you want a full-service offering and want a provider to create additional value for your business, then you need to determine which of these providers match your business and personal style best to get the maximum sale value. You must choose a provider that can deliver enhanced value and is willing to create a structure and process that suits you and your business. As you may expect, you will pay more for the providers that can create this additional value. Still, you should consider it not as a cost but as an investment to build a more valuable business. In addition, a significant proportion of the higher fees are usually performance-based, so they will only be paid when there is a successful business sale.

If you think of a business sale like an iceberg, the part most people associate with getting the best price is only the negotiation itself, which is incorrect. While being a strong negotiator is essential to getting a reasonable price, if the business has weak areas, no matter how skilled the negotiator is, an intelligent buyer will uncover those areas and bring the price down accordingly or withdraw from the process entirely. As you can see from the following diagram, the negotiation is just the tip of the iceberg. Look at all the aspects of what constitutes value in a business. You will see that many items must come together to create value that prospective purchasers are prepared to pay. This list is not extensive, and numerous subsets exist within each category. Still, it should give you an understanding of what must be considered when creating value.

'Iceberg view' of where the value lies in a business sale

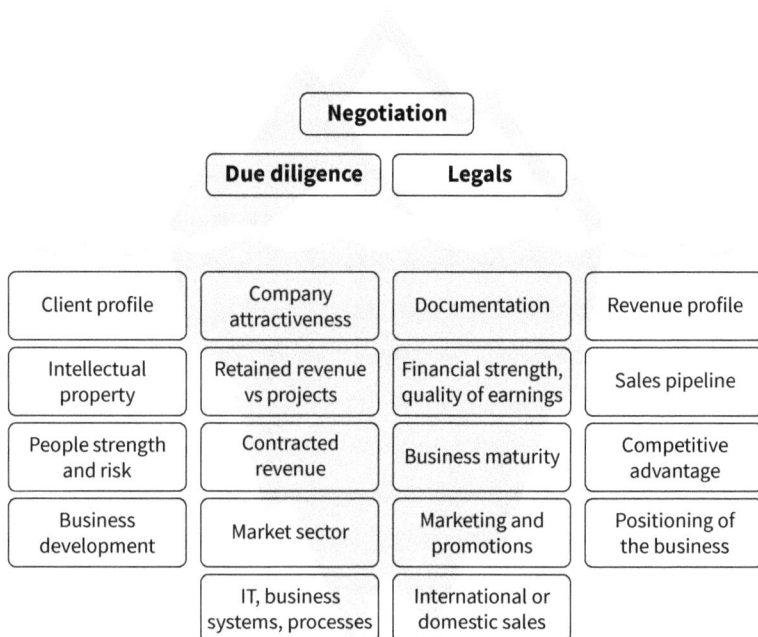

	Negotiation		
	Due diligence	**Legals**	
Client profile	Company attractiveness	Documentation	Revenue profile
Intellectual property	Retained revenue vs projects	Financial strength, quality of earnings	Sales pipeline
People strength and risk	Contracted revenue	Business maturity	Competitive advantage
Business development	Market sector	Marketing and promotions	Positioning of the business
	IT, business systems, processes	International or domestic sales	

What is clear is that there are many more items a business needs to get right and in place than just a good negotiation process. It is also true that some things need significant time and effort to correct; they can't just be fixed at the 11th hour. For example, if the client profile of a business is not optimal, there needs to be a proper evaluation, a clear strategy to improve it, a detailed action plan and nine to 12 months to execute the strategy and show results.

A. Corporate advisor

In the broadest sense, an advisor provides advice and opinions, so a corporate advisor or corporate advisory company will focus primarily on advising an organisation on activities like buying, selling or merging businesses and any other transactions that involve a change of ownership.

In Australia, these can range from single operators (though unlikely to offer a wide range of services) to large, multi-national organisations. They should be able to provide a strategic review of the business and deliver a plan to increase the value of the business. However, you should determine if the advisor will provide a 'delivery solution' for the strategic plan as some of the larger advisors are unable or not prepared to provide those services for smaller businesses. Ironically, a smaller corporate advisor will have the cost structure and flexibility to provide a strategy delivery service, providing they have the experience that you need. In summary, once you have determined that a corporate advisor is the best option for you, you then need to ensure they are the most effective/relevant to provide the required solution.

B. Global banking and financial services firms

Global banking and financial services firms will only apply to larger and more profitable organisations if the exit path is for an Initial Public Offering (IPO), otherwise known as a stock market listing. They provide a complete end-to-end service, including raising finance, tax advice, exposure to global markets, etc., so their fees reflect the full range of services. Like a corporate advisor, they will add strategic advice. Still, given the typical size of businesses in Australia, there will not be many companies large enough to warrant the size and structure of fees that these providers will charge. In reality, their structures and overheads are not suited for small- to medium-sized businesses.

C. Big-tier consultancy firms

Big-tier consultancy firms have similar offerings to the big banks, and they continue to develop their range of products and services to offer a fully comprehensive service. While they offer funding advice, they will not provide funding directly. Due to their global presence and range of products and services, they will typically serve medium to large businesses and are stronger in international sales. Again, they provide strategic advice as well as manage the transaction. While there will be more companies that can use their services, it is still mainly larger companies that can afford their fees or suit their model.

2. Transaction services

If your preference is for a quick sale and you are not concerned with increasing the value of your business, a pure transaction service would probably best suit your needs. Several options available to you are from different professions/providers but are all capable of delivering a transaction service. The fees for this service will be lower than those charged for the 'strategic services' and are more likely to be a fee based on work completed than for a successful outcome (though not always). You should consider using these providers if you want an immediate sale, do not wish to increase the value of your business and are confident that your business is already 'sale ready'.

D. Business broker

Business brokers are transaction specialists. They do not provide value-enhancing/value-adding strategy products or services. They are focused on working through the practical items in a transaction. Any broker who has completed many transactions will have a model or process they follow and should know how to manage a sales process. Most brokers work independently or with a partner and so may have limited capacity. Ideally, you should find one qualified and accredited by an organisation such as the Australian Institute of Business Brokers (AIBB). While their fees may be less overall than a corporate advisor, they will have a similar fee structure and not be significantly cheaper for the transaction element of the sales process.

E. Accountant or lawyer

Owners usually only use an accountant or lawyer to sell a business if they have had a long-standing relationship and, therefore, know and trust their work. Most medium-size accountancy and legal firms manage the transaction themselves and, like a broker, provide a professional service but not additional value (e.g. deliver a growth plan). They may not be a strong negotiator either. They are likely less experienced than businesses that only specialise in buying or selling businesses. An advantage of engaging your accounting firm to manage the sale is that they will know all the details of your financials and present them clearly and professionally. Your legal firm should know the history behind the business, which will be helpful when deciding the best sale vehicle for you and preparing or amending a sale or business purchase agreement.

F. Online agencies

Online agencies are, in effect, an online shop window for a business. The owner will complete basic information on their business to populate a generic template. The agencies then distribute it to their database. They then manage the initial responses before introducing the potential buyers to the seller. While this would be the cheapest way to sell your business, you will probably receive the least value through this channel and minimal support if negotiations get challenging. This type of service should only be used for businesses that are ready for sale, simple and easy to understand and where there is a known market need. Owners should expect many time-wasters, and they will have to manage most of the process themselves. Confidentiality can also be difficult to control, purely due to the broad marketing of the business.

G. Do-it-yourself (DIY)

If a business owner has been through a sales process before or they are dealing with a professional buyer, they may feel they can manage the sale themselves, supported by hired specialists such as legal and financial when required. It can certainly be done, but there are many areas you need to be aware of when making this decision.

1. As someone who has run the business for several years, you are unlikely to change much or anything about it as you prepare it for sale. If you had seen areas to add value, you would have already implemented them, so it is unlikely

that you will be increasing the value of the business in the sales process.

2. It will be a significant distraction for you. Even when you know the details of the process, selling a business is a considerable time commitment. As you will see later in the book, when I detail the process, there are many steps and stakeholders to manage, all of whom need feeding with information. If you manage it yourself, all information flow must come from you. Given that a typical sales process will be between six and 12 months, who will run the business and keep profits and sales as high as possible through this critical time?

3. Unless you have a heart of stone, selling a business is an emotional event for most business owners. You and your family will have sacrificed many things and heavily invested much of yourselves to make your business successful. You will have employees, clients and suppliers whom you have known well throughout the years, and many will be friends. Selling a business is hard enough; selling it yourself and dealing with the emotions as well is very challenging. In addition, when it comes to areas where you need to remain unemotional (for example, negotiating the sales price), you need to be detached and not take it personally when you are offered a low price or a prospective buyer picks out flaws in the business. A negotiator's view mustn't be clouded or compromised by emotion.

4. 'You don't know what you don't know'. If you don't know your way through a sales process or learnt the 'tricks of the trade', there will be many opportunities for an experienced

buyer to pay less for your business. If the buyer is also inexperienced, you may both miss something important. Inevitably, the whole process will take much longer and cause issues later, even after the sale.

As you can see, there are several support options for you to pick from. While there are many factors to take into consideration, an owner should ask themselves two critical questions:

1. Which option is most likely to get me a successful sale?
2. Which option will increase the value of my business and get me the highest price?

This is important because those options that provide value-increasing services and a higher chance of completing the transaction will have higher costs that will be reflected in their price structures. For example, there is no point in expecting to get the services of a professional corporate advisor for the same fees as a business broker. You should do your due diligence on whom you select; their fees should only be one aspect. What you must evaluate is what is the likely Return on Investment (ROI) of the fees. For example, if a corporate advisor charges you $300K more than a business broker but achieves an additional $3M on the sales price, which should you choose?

The following chart illustrates three aspects of what you will likely get from which service provider. They are:

- The X-axis demonstrates the likelihood that the relevant service provider will increase the value of a business through its sales process. The further to the right, the more likely they are to add value.

- The Y-axis shows the comparative levels of costs or fees that each provider would charge for their services. The higher up the axis, the more they will charge.

- The size of each 'bubble' shows the likelihood of a successful sale. The bigger the bubble, the bigger the chance of a successful sale.

The chart is viewed through the lens of the total number of businesses available for sale and so will be skewed towards the small- to medium-sized business market.

Three dimensions of various service providers

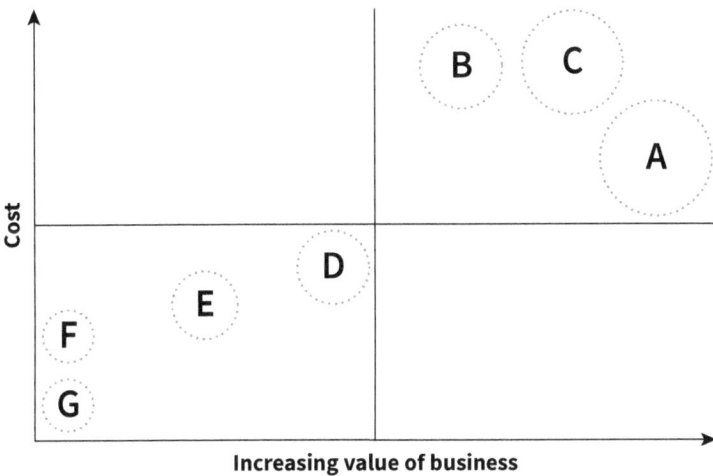

Increasing value of business

Chart key:
A. Corporate advisor
B. Global banking and financial services firm
C. Big-tier consulting firm
D. Business broker
E. Accountant or lawyer
F. Online agency
G. DIY

The following are some observations from the chart:

- A will provide the highest chance of success, create the most value and be the third most expensive option.
- B and C are the most expensive options and have a good chance of success, but C will probably add more value to a business than B.
- D will have a similar chance of success as B, be cheaper than A, B or C, but add much less value to a business than A, B or C.
- E will be cheaper than D but add less value and have less likelihood of a successful sale.
- F and G will not add any additional value to your business in the process and have a much higher chance of being unsuccessful in a sale, but be the cheapest option.

The above points are highly subjective and purely my personal opinion. I have ranked each provider as I see the market, which, as I previously commented, is heavily skewed (in terms of numbers of businesses) to the small- and medium-sized businesses in Australia. It is key to understand that if you break down the market into more specific categories (e.g. businesses with revenue over $100M), providers B and C will rate much higher because that is their area of focus and specialty. When there is a business of this size, they can afford to pay much higher monthly retainer fees, allowing both the banking institutions and big consulting firms to allocate more resources to the account.

Once you have selected the type of provider you believe best suits your needs, you need to determine which organisation or individual you feel has the necessary experience and capability to deliver what they promise. It is a critical decision, so you should take the time and effort to make the most informed choice possible. Fundamentally, you must choose someone you trust with one of your most valuable assets, who will represent you and your business to the outside world and protect and keep you safe and sane through the process. Finally, try to find someone you like and with whom you can still work with if (more likely when!) things go wrong in the process.

CHAPTER 3

WHY DOES IT SO OFTEN END IN TEARS?

For every business sale process that concludes in a successful transaction, there will be many more that do not. How can that be? Even a logical, rational person who knows this is the most critical transaction of their business lives and does everything possible to make it successful won't always succeed. There can be numerous causes for this, and any event (or a combination of events) can contribute to the failure. The key ones are outlined in the following sections.

Procrastination

We all do it. Though there are thousands of books on 'How to get things done', we continue to overthink, make lists and have great ideas and we just don't get things done. Many organisations of all shapes and sizes have spent significant time and money research-ing and creating detailed strategic plans that never get executed.

There has never been a better time in history to be in a world where you can quickly find the information you need to do something, but still, we don't. That is because it is hard. We are built to run on autopilot. Whenever we have something to do that is big and scary or unknown, most people will find all the reasons *not to* instead of *to do*. When it comes to selling a business, it is a big step for an owner to get started. It is even harder to make it a priority every day until the business is sold, which is what it takes – progress every single day to accomplish the thousands of tasks you need to complete to get over the finish line.

Lack of preparedness for the sale process

Selling a business is complex and challenging, requiring many things to happen in parallel and harmoniously. For a business to successfully transfer from one owner to another, it helps the process significantly if it is professionally prepared for sale. This includes ensuring that the required financial records are correct and up to date and accurately portray the performance of the business. A private business will have set up its financial and tax reporting for the benefit and preferences of an owner. It may have items that should be excluded or included in the financial reports to give an accurate picture of the business. For example, many business owners own the premises they operate their business from, and they may not be charging the business rent for the property, as they see it as just charging themselves. However, suppose the business needs that property to produce its goods or services. In that case, the financial statements need to show the impact of commercial rent on the business post-sale. A key area for a business to ensure it is up to date and squeaky clean is documented superannuation payments for all employees and all relevant taxes. If either of these is not up to date, it will immediately trigger alarm bells for a prospective buyer.

It will also include non-financial areas such as succession planning for the current owner(s), and if any training and development plans have been implemented for key staff, etc. A prepared business should have all the information a prospective buyer will require, well-structured and complete before the sale process commences, ideally in an electronic data room. If it isn't, it dramatically increases the time of the sales process, and time (as detailed on page 43) kills many potential acquisitions. It can either give the owner the upper hand if it is well prepared or cause the potential buyer nervousness about the reliability of the business, causing them to go cold.

Emotional

Selling a business is probably the most emotional thing a business owner can do (outside of getting married, having children or buying a home). In many cases, they have built it from scratch with no money, no income and many difficult years to navigate. Any business owner will relate to this; we've all had our journeys and challenges. Unsurprisingly, it is often a highly emotional event when it comes time to sell. This vast area cannot be given justice in this section alone, or indeed this book (it may well be the topic of another!); however, it is one of the principal reasons a potential transaction may fail. A seller's or buyer's emotions will be what they are: personal and built upon their values and experiences. It can be challenging for a business owner not to get defensive when a third party asks detailed questions about their business and finds things that are not quite right. It is in the best interests of a prospective buyer to find fault with a business before buying it, giving them the flexibility to negotiate the price or, if they find a serious issue, pull out of the acquisition altogether. The best way both parties can avoid emotions stalling a sale is to engage professional and trusted advisors who will take an unemotional (hopefully empathic) view of the many challenges along the way and keep their party on course. When choosing an advisor, part of your assessment of them should include their communication style and manner – will they remain calm and in control in the most emotional of times, including managing and advising you when you are troubled and about to throw in the towel?

Buying a business can also be an emotional event for a buyer, particularly one who has not done it before. Acquiring a business could mean they are taking on significant debt, postponing the family holiday, or just feeling out of their depth. Therefore, we are looking at a technically challenging and emotional event for both parties.

Differences of opinion on valuation

It is unlikely that both a buyer and seller will view (and therefore value) a business exactly the same. Apart from any technical differences (even qualified accountants can disagree on the most appropriate methodology to value the same business), there is the lens that each party looks through based on their experience and understanding of the business at that point in time and indeed looking forward. A seller starts with a positive view of the things that have helped grow the business and the income it has provided over its life. A buyer will be looking at the business as it is today before they can add any future value, the reasons why it may not be worth the initial assessment and what risks they are assuming in the future.

That is how both parties start. If, after the presentation of the initial information, the buyer does not satisfy their immediate fears, then it is unlikely they will even submit an NBIO. These underlying views do not change and can re-ignite anytime during the process. Even if there is a top-level 'agreement', any initial concerns can work as a 'hard reset' and take either party's position back to the start.

It is worth understanding here the main ways a business can be valued. To make it more complicated, different countries have different preferred methods, so if you have an international buyer, do not be surprised if they want to value your business using a method (or accounting standard) you may never have heard of. There are several reasons why different methods are used, but below are four of the more common ones in Australia:

1. Multiple method. This can be a multiple of EBITDA, net profit or revenue.

2. Discounted Cash Flow (DCF).

3. Market valuation.

4. Adjusted Net Asset Value (NAV).

It is important to understand each method's key components and the value of your business under each. When it comes to selling your business, you should be attempting to get the buyer to value your business on the method that will provide the highest value for you, or at the very least, a fair and reasonable method, even if it isn't your preferred choice. Most business owners, if they haven't been through many business sales before, are unlikely to have encountered some of these methods, so you should get professional guidance to ensure you understand them and how to apply them.

1. Multiple method

This is the most common valuation method used in Australia, with about 70% of all business transactions using a form of this method. One of the main reasons is its simplicity and ease at which an agreed value can be achieved. The multiple method consists of two numbers that produce a value for a business when multiplied together. These are:

1. One of either EBITDA, net profit or revenue

2. A coefficient range that represents the relevant value of your industry sector (typically a range of numbers) and where the buyer views your business within that range.

The two numbers are then multiplied together, creating the valuation price. For example, let's say a company produced a normalised EBITDA in the last financial year (normalised means adjusted for exceptional and non-recurring items, expenses and revenue) of $5 million. It operates in a traditional manufacturing sector where the historical multiple range for a business of its size in that industry is 3–5 times. This will result in a valuation range of between $15M and $25M. As you can see, this is a wide variation and where the debate (and often disagreement) is, 'What is the exact multiple that will be applied?'. Many factors determine where an individual company should sit in a valuation range (this is covered more fully later in the book). But for now, let's assume both parties agree that a multiple of 4 is a fair reflection of the company, giving a valuation of $20M (EBITDA of $5M × 4).

Using this method avoids the need for valuing the company's balance sheet items at the point of making an NBIO (though these will be reviewed and considered by a prospective buyer as part of due diligence). The balance sheet is often treated as 'debt free–cash free', meaning the seller must deal with outstanding liabilities and take any surplus cash, apart from those liabilities and assets that are required to deliver the current and projected trading results, e.g. work-in-progress, supplier liabilities for future work to be delivered, etc.

One of the disadvantages of this method is that it typically looks backward in time, and as we all know, historical performance is not necessarily an accurate predictor of future value.

2. Discounted Cash Flow (DCF)

DCF is considered by many to be the most accurate valuation method for a business and is often the preferred choice for professional acquirers, accountants, etc. Its strength lies in that it factors both the future earning potential of a business and the associated risk. Another advantage over other methods is that it looks to future performance and can be used on established businesses and start-ups. It can also equally work on both small and large businesses. A DCF consists of three key elements:

1. Cash flow from the business over a set (future) period.
2. A discount rate is applied to the future cash flows to factor in the risk of not achieving 100% of the theoretical cash flows.
3. Terminal or future exit value. This focuses on the probable value at the end of the DCF period and what a potential buyer may achieve if it were to sell it at that moment.

3. Market valuation

This is based on two sources of comparative valuations:

1. Comparable transactions. As you might expect, this method looks at what similar businesses to yours have been bought for.

2. Public company valuations. This compares your business to the current value of publicly listed companies with an equivalent business model (discounted for relative size).

4. Adjusted Net Asset Value (NAV)

This balance sheet–focused valuation method is appropriate for valuing a business with significant balance sheet items. Therefore, it is unsuitable to value service-based businesses or those with few physical assets.

As you can see, a business can be valued in several ways and, depending on the method, can produce widely differing valuations. A sophisticated buyer may use two or three methods to value a business and pick the most appropriate or a combination of methods to produce their valuation. This can confuse a seller who has never sold a business or is not financially strong. I strongly recommend you have an expert to help you in this area. If you haven't engaged with an advisor, I would suggest engaging an accountant or advisor experienced in business valuations so they may guide you through the process and ensure the valuation method is appropriate for your business and that the potential buyer has applied it correctly. You simply cannot afford to be ill-informed or naïve regarding how your business is valued.

And I haven't even mentioned the emotional reasons why a seller will value a business differently from a buyer.

Due diligence issues

So, you have gone through the initial information stages, received an NBIO and successfully negotiated the NBIO to your satisfaction. Now, you get into due diligence. In short, due diligence is where a potential buyer will request (and you will need to supply) detailed information regarding your business, and I mean detailed information. The buyer and their team have limited time to ensure they haven't missed anything and confirm their valuation. They will ask for every conceivable piece of information on the business and, if they do their job properly, should have plenty of questions. There is a good probability that they could either reduce their offer or withdraw completely if the questions on material issues are not answered to their satisfaction. There will always be issues in due diligence, but how they are dealt with is what matters. Even the trickiest of issues can be negated and even turned into a positive outcome if they are professionally and adequately addressed. However, the opposite is also true; if poorly handled, even the slightest issue can lead to mistrust and further digging.

Many issues in due diligence can (with planning and preparation) be predicted and remedial action taken. You are legally bound to disclose anything of a material nature fully, and you are not to mislead or lie about anything, even if it stops the deal from going ahead.

As you can see, there is plenty of opportunity in a due diligence process for a deal to come unstuck. It is undoubtedly one of the longest and most complicated parts of the process. Careful management of the process and ensuring all questions are logged correctly, responded to and completed is critical. It is a highly significant time commitment and distraction.

Unsaleability or transferability of a business

Once the sales process has begun and detailed information is provided, the buyer may uncover that the business, in their opinion, is unbuyable. While it may have provided you with a good income for many years, the business or a good proportion of its value is not transferable for various reasons.

This is not the buyer's fault; the seller should have had an unemotional, detailed valuation assessment of their business before entering into any sales process. This valuation/review of the business should go well beyond the financials and cover all the items needed to be in place to ensure the business is saleable/ transferrable.

There are two main areas where a buyer would deem the business to be non-transferable:

1. The current owner is an integral part of the business. Most business owners are expected to play a leading role in their business, and buyers are fine with that; they would be surprised if that weren't the case. They are also ordinarily agreeable to a post-sale transition period where the owner keeps working in the business to ensure a safe transfer of knowledge, clients, etc. In fact, many buyers request it. However, they will not be comfortable if they observe an unhealthy reliance on an owner for the majority of either revenue or profit generation or for running the business in general. Key signals are an owner working excessive hours, not taking adequate holidays, no apparent delegated authority to staff, etc.

2. The client base is not secured and/or there is too much reliance on one or two key clients. While a buyer would not necessarily want to see thousands of clients, they also do not want to see an over-reliance on one or two clients. If, for example, the top two clients of a business make up 50% of the revenue, if those clients were to leave the business at any

time, half of the revenue and probably the majority of the profit would disappear. The risk is even higher for a buyer if those clients are not contracted. A buyer will spend a lot of time understanding and asking questions about revenue and clients, as it is critical to the value of any business. Retaining key clients and revenue are probably the central aspects of your business they will lose most sleep about.

Change of buyer's (or seller's) plans

Things happen in a buyer's life that may have nothing to do with the seller's business. Suppose they are a large or public company. In that case, they will review multiple options at any point, and something else may require all their attention and/or resources. In smaller businesses, the buyer may have suddenly run into some commercial pressures, or they may have some personal issues that they have to deal with. Remember, while you both agreed on an NBIO in good faith, it is not binding, and until it becomes such, either party can withdraw at any time (for no good reason). It can be very frustrating when this happens. Still, it does occur and is one of the reasons why, in the early stages, at least, you should have more than one interested party in the process. A professional advisor is critical to keeping other parties and 'Plan Bs' warm and ready to utilise if anything happens and 'Plan A' withdraws.

Buyer buys a different business

That's right. The buyer may have been looking at a similar business, even a close competitor, at the same time and decided to buy it instead. If they are a large business and an experienced buyer, they will have probably conducted extensive market research into several businesses within your sector and approached several businesses simultaneously. If you think about it from their point of view, they will not know the details of any of those businesses or what owners may accept as an offer until they start a process. Even worse, depending on where you get to with them in the process, they may now know significant details about your business. How well covered were you with your confidentiality agreement? Did you provide more information than was required at any particular point? There is no doubt this is a risk you run when you decide to sell your business, and it is another area that you and/or your advisor should have done some work on before you disclose too much information.

While they may not openly disclose that they are speaking with another party, there are often tell-tale signs. A good advisor will watch for any signal that a potential buyer is more interested elsewhere and gather any market intelligence they can to confirm.

The best way to avoid this (assuming your business was well prepared) is to move as swiftly through all the stages as possible, as once you have agreed on an NBIO, it is your deal to lose, so you and your advisor should be pushing the pace and certainly leading by example by the speed you respond to any requests.

Time

Probably the greatest deal-killer of all is time. If too much time is taken to move from one stage to the next, or in total, then one party can (and often does) pull up stumps.

I believe the worst, most inexcusable thing either party can do in a sales process is to take too much time, which can be for several (most not valid, in my opinion) reasons. In short, you either want to sell, or you want to buy. If you need to slow things down or pause at any time in the process, you should say so and let everyone get on with what they have to do next. A good advisor will not allow time to drift between stages unless there is an agreed delay for a reason declared and accepted.

From a seller's point of view, selling your business should be a life-changing event; why would you not put your heart and soul into it and put in the required hours? This should be the same for your advisor, and one of the reasons why a significant part of their fees should be performance-based and sizeable enough for them to do whatever it takes to complete a deal.

No two business sales are the same, and there are many reasons why the time it takes to sell varies so much. There are numerous participants in a sale process, all of whom could (and do) go off the boil occasionally. It can take anything from three to 12 months, and what I would say is if you are truly serious about maximising the sale price for your business, then you should give a corporate advisor at least nine to 12 months to not only professionally prepare the business for a sale but to give them time to find the hidden value in your business. As you will have seen from my six-stage process, the more time I can have with a business, the more value I can add.

People lie

I realise this may come as a shock to some of you, but some people lie! They lie under oath, to their spouses and during the sales process. Now, it may not always be an out-and-out lie, but if there is something that either party would prefer the other didn't know, they may not declare it or try to camouflage it a bit. This can also happen when multiple shareholders are not honest with each other. I have seen deals blow up simply because one of the shareholders has not wanted to sell. They couldn't tell their business partners, so they sabotaged the deal and found any reason to stop the sale.

As I mentioned earlier, you are legally bound to tell the truth and not hide anything of material value or interest to a buyer. So tell the truth and check on any joint owners that they are too.

Funding

You would be surprised how far down a sales process some sellers will go and how much time and information they provide to a prospective buyer without checking if the buyer has the funds to pay for the company and, indeed, if they intend to phase any part of the settlement amount. For example, if a seller will not budge on receiving 100% of the transaction value on completion and the buyer can only afford 50% at completion and intends to pay the balance in 12 months' time, it is much better to have that discussion up front rather than at the end. The other area that an inexperienced buyer may not realise is the impact on their finances of funding the working capital of a new business. It is there in every business, but in some, it can be a significant amount of cash that may have to be funded for a period.

You should ask the questions upfront regarding a buyer's capacity to pay, how they intend to fund the acquisition (i.e. how much out of their own cash and how much through debt), and test them to see if they have correctly calculated the amount of working capital the business will need from the financials you provided. Have they been preapproved if they fund part or all of it through debt? You should also be discussing with them when the payment(s) will be made – are they going to give you 100% on completion, or is there an element deferred or dependent on future performance?

Legals

There are lawyers, and then there are lawyers. Both parties will need one, and one of the party's lawyers will take the lead in producing the initial draft sale agreement document. From then, the document will be reviewed countless times. If either side has a weak or difficult lawyer, especially if teamed with an inexperienced buyer or seller, then this could easily be a deal stopper.

There are always issues over the legals. It is a critical part of the process, and the sale agreement is a vital document to complete. In addition to having sound legal counsel, you also need a solid commercial view of the sale agreement, as lawyers cannot sort everything. Ideally, a business person is the best person to give this commercial view. The challenge for business owners is that while they will have business sense, they may be inexperienced in reading and modifying legal documents. This experience is critical. It can rarely be delegated to anyone else in the company. So, if it isn't going to be the business owner, it needs to be one of the professional advisors with solid commercial experience and business sense. Legals are one of the critical areas that take up time, partly because of the nature of the work and the importance of getting it right and partly because the documents and associated questions have to go back and forth between both parties. Time delays can occur simply because someone hasn't processed a task allocated to them.

Post-sale requirements

These will be flushed out in the legal process but will include items such as the requirement for an owner to stay working in the business for a period, warranties required of the seller and any post-sale restraints. Some of these can be quite onerous and restrictive and can cause a deal to come unstuck even if most of the deal has been agreed upon. For example, do you want to work in the business for up to two years, reporting to someone else? The buyer may want or need you to, or they will not complete the deal. What will you do if you want out after three months of a 24-month commitment but have an earnout payment linked to the performance of the business post-sale?

Post-sale requirements/requests may seem onerous or unreasonable. You need to determine if the buyer is overly cautious/difficult or has a good reason for their request. Again, a lawyer will look at it through a legal lens, and it will also help if both parties have open commercial discussions regarding the reason behind post-sale requirements.

CHAPTER 4

HOW LONG DOES IT TAKE?

There are various statistics about how long the sales process takes. Still, a commonly held view among advisors is that it is about 11 months from start to finish. Does it need to take this long? Not if a business is well prepared for sale by a professional advisor and the buyer is experienced and has funding in place. If both parties determine a thorough review of the business and produce a comprehensive set of legals in a short time frame, given the size of the business, it can take anywhere from six to 12 weeks. However, a business sale is rarely that quick. In my experience, a more realistic time frame would be six to nine months.

The reason for this significant amount of time? Sometimes, it can be for legitimate reasons, but most of the time, it is because there is no detailed, time-based plan that someone drives and holds all parties to account.

It is a complicated process with numerous information requests and legal questions to address. If the information is not readily available or the time taken to respond is not immediate, significant delays can incur while waiting for the other party's response to a request.

In addition, there are often multiple stakeholders, all of whom need managing to keep the process moving along.

In my opinion, gaining the maximum value for a business will take more than a year (of 'value-add' time). However, please note that this is a very different use of time than I have just described. It may help to think of the time in a sales process in two different ways:

1. **Value-add time.** This is the time needed to build value in a business. As I will explain in detail in the six-stage EBITDA+™ SIX STEPS TO SUCCESS process, to maximise the value of a business, it needs to:

   a. be evaluated as it is today

   b. understand what its maximum value could be

   c. build a plan that will deliver that increase in value

   d. execute the plan

   e. professionally prepare all the documents and information required for a data room.

   All of this is 'good' time in my opinion. As long as the process I have highlighted is being actioned, the time taken is required for the value to be delivered. Of course, it shouldn't be open-ended, as if not careful, 'good' time can turn into 'bad' time.

2. **Transaction time.** This is the time required to do the mechanics of selling a business. This should be as concise as possible, given that it has to be professionally managed with defined processes and documents to be adhered to. Any delay or procrastination (for no good reason) is 'bad'

time and should be eliminated. Delays are a killer, and as discussed, one of the key reasons deals sometimes don't proceed. Simply put, a sales transaction process can be very defined with a list of tasks that must be completed. If both parties allocate enough focus and resources, momentum will be maintained, and there should be minimal time delay.

Another reason to take the time required to prepare a business before engaging in a sales process is to ensure that all the documents are available, reviewed and ready to share with a prospective buyer. This significantly reduces the time required in the transaction phase and increases the chances of completing the transaction successfully.

CHAPTER 5

HOW MUCH IS MY BUSINESS WORTH?

'Beauty is in the eye of the beholder', or in this context, the value of a business is as each party sees it.

No buyer, no matter how well they do their due diligence, will ever know the history and intricate details of a seller's business. Likewise, even if they work with their buyer for two years, no seller will ever fully know or understand the buyer's business or motivations. They approach the transaction from opposite ends of the spectrum; therefore, it is almost impossible for them ever to be completely aligned on the value of the business.

They are also looking at it for different purposes. A seller is predictably looking to maximise the financial value they will get from the transaction with as few conditions or time delays as possible. On the other hand, the buyer will not just be looking to minimise the amount they pay but also trying to evaluate potential synergies within their own business after acquiring it and identify any risks they may be assuming. They may also like to defer some of the payment on completion (for example, to assist with cash flow, reduce any debt required, etc.) and even have some of the purchase price be conditional on the business performance for the first 12–24 months post-completion.

So, we have several hurdles to overcome when attempting to gain common ground on a transaction price:

- **Total financial value.** The top-line value of a business. Before any discussions, a seller will probably already know the range they would accept for their business. A minimum 'walk-away' figure and an ideal 'immediately sell before they change their mind' figure. A buyer probably won't have enough information before a process has begun to determine what the business may be worth. Still, they will certainly have a budget figure and a maximum they can afford to pay. Of course, they won't disclose this (unless they do so as a negotiating tactic). However, it is helpful for a seller to know this number and the amount a potential buyer has paid for similar businesses.

- **Valuation method selected.** I explained four common valuation methods, but there also are several others. The buyer and seller will have their preferred methodology, so some common ground must be reached before agreeing to a financial number. An experienced buyer may also use two or three different methods to compare the results and adopt the one favouring their position. It is not unusual for an inexperienced seller to have no preconceived ideas or knowledge of the various methods to value a business and so leave it up to the buyer. I would always say that a seller should know very clearly how they would want their business valued, even if it has to be negotiated.

- **Amount paid on completion.** Buyers would prefer deferring an amount, ideally with some performance conditions attached. Sellers would like 100% paid on completion, ideally with no conditions. While this may sound like a methodology point, it goes to why a buyer may undervalue or appear to undervalue the business in the eyes of a seller. In reality, the buyer may not undervalue the business at all but needs some form of deferred structure to either afford the deal and/or offset some risk.

- **Any deferred amounts that are conditional on the performance of the business post-completion.** This is part of the point above. The buyer and seller may see the business's total purchase price as the same. Let's use, for example, a purchase price of $20M. However, they may still value the business differently because the seller wants all $20M to be paid on completion, while the buyer has requested $5M be deferred over two years based on the financial performance of the business. In this example, the seller may view the offer as only $15M, counting the $5M as an additional amount to be earned, excluding it from their view of the current value. On the other hand, the buyer sees that they are still potentially paying $20M for the business, valuing the transaction as such. The buyer has structured their offer so that they only pay the full $20M if the business performs in line with that $20M valuation. Note that performance-based payment structures can cause many issues for both parties and must be well thought through and structured to be used effectively and fairly.

- **Remuneration for the owner if it is a requirement that they work in the business for a period post-sale.** While this isn't strictly part of the valuation of the business, I have included it here as often a seller will consider that it is. They are used to viewing what income the business delivers every year for them, not distinguishing the remuneration and profit distributions split, as they both currently go to them. All that changes post-sale, of course, and the seller will (probably) not be entitled to any share of profit distributions. They may look at the remuneration offered to cover some of the amount they were used to receiving from profits. There is also an emotional element to what the buyer offers the seller as their remuneration. If the seller deems it too low, they may take it as a negative view of their personal worth to the new owner.

- **Non-financial aspects of the business.** This is covered in detail later in the book, and to get a quick overview of what items may be included as the non-financial aspects that affect an offer price, look at the 'iceberg' diagram in Chapter 2. As I explained, the non-financial aspects of a business play a significant part in calculating an offer, particularly if the 'multiple method' is used.

SECTION 2

I CAN'T DO THIS

CHAPTER 6

I NEED MORE MONEY THAN WHAT I HAVE BEEN OFFERED

This book is about how to significantly increase your business value and realise that value in a sales event, it isn't aimed at those businesses that may be financially struggling. Still, I felt it appropriate to cover it to an extent in this chapter as there can be quite sizeable businesses with unsustainable balance sheets for their business's current profitability and value. While businesses in that situation have added complexities and challenges, a good part of the process is similar. Many of them are also saleable and attractive to prospective purchasers. The issue can be that the net funds from the sale (after all balance sheet items) are insufficient for the owner to meet all of their obligations and financial requirements from the sale.

This is a more complicated issue than it may first appear. First, let's distinguish between what an owner may *wish* for and what they *need*. You need to forget what you wish for (irrelevant and irrational) and focus on what the business is worth and what you need. These two aspects are the critical two viewpoints that must align. For example, if you need $10M from the sale of your business to clear your debts and provide you with an income for retirement, and the business is worth $14M, you are in a great position. However, suppose you need $10M, and the business is only worth $8M. In that case, it is unlikely that even the world's greatest negotiator will get you an additional $2M just from the negotiation process. You need to be more creative and find ways to increase the value of the business before you sell (or pay down debt if the business has it). Therefore, it is important to get advice (the *right* type of advice); the earlier, the better, ideally at least two years before you want to sell. This can be, and often is, a reason why a realistic and fair offer for a business may get rejected. When the current owner looks at all the liabilities they have to pay out and what they need post-sale for themselves, the maths just doesn't add up. I have met a number of business owners ready to sell but haven't managed to get their business into a position where they can because of this issue. If nothing is done, the result is that they are unable to ever sell the business and realise its fair value.

This is when a good, experienced (strategic) advisor can help. If they have experience in running businesses, not just advising them, they will have the understanding and capability to work with an owner to grow the value of the business and even help them financially restructure it. The one clear thing is that doing nothing is not an option, as the owner will inevitably become disheartened and lose focus, and the business's performance will suffer. It doesn't take much once that has happened for a financially challenged business to slip into trouble quickly. I have seen four businesses, all of significant size and with keen buyers, who, for several reasons (lack of knowledge, drive, etc.), fell into this trap and end up in administration with no value and significant post-administration debt issues for the owner. Please do not allow yourself to get into this position. If you think that there may be a risk that your business may not yield the amount you need from a sale event, you should consider the following:

1. Get your business professionally assessed/valued as it is today. Use either a corporate advisor or an independent business valuer.

2. Determine what all your net liabilities are (liabilities net of assets). Again, I recommend getting a professional accountant, advisor or business valuer to do this for you, even if you believe you know all your net liabilities.

3. Establish the gap. Quite simply, deduct your net liabilities from the current valuation (as produced above). This will inform you how much more you need to get from selling your business.

4. Get professional help to build a solid strategic plan and an achievable business roadmap.

5. Execute the plan consistently.

6. Get the business reassessed once you have completed all of the actions on the plan to see if a sale would now realise the amount you need to clear your net liabilities (and any surplus you may need).

I know I have made the above sound very simple. If you are in this position, you may be saying, 'It's easy for him to say,' but as hard as it may be, you need to do something different, and it is never too soon to start.

CHAPTER 7

WHERE DO I START?

I know it is hard. If you have never sold a business before, where do you start? Who do you speak with first, a lawyer, an accountant or a corporate advisor? Do you put an advert online or in the newspaper? Do you start calling people who may be interested in buying your business and take it from there?

As in most walks of life, a typical process can be followed, but it isn't a straight line. Think back to other significant events in your life, such as getting married, having children, buying a home or setting up a business. You didn't know how to do any of those things the first time, so have faith that you are more than capable of doing this. It will not be a straightforward journey; the path will zig and zag, and there will be many hills and valleys to navigate. The key is to speak with an individual or company that has bought and sold many businesses. A good advisor will take time to learn your business and what you need to get out of the sale and then build a bespoke plan for you. However, if you select a simple 'transactionist', they will give you a prescriptive plan that you must follow to the letter. Both will get you started and take you on the journey. We described the different types of organisations that can help you sell your business in Chapter 2.

The thing is, you just have to take action. Thinking about selling your business will not get you started. Decide what type of support you need, make contact and have the initial meeting. It won't cost you anything (apart from your time), and at the end of one meeting, you should have a more informed view of what to do next.

I would strongly advise you not to start discussions with current stakeholders (apart from any other owners/directors) or prospective acquirers unless you know the process you will follow. If you have personal experience and understand what you are doing, I still suggest you have an exploratory meeting with a strategic corporate advisor who will explain their services. You can then decide whether to engage them or explore other providers. If you have not sold a business before, start speaking to the types of providers you think you might want to engage. Regardless of your personal experience and knowledge, it is critical that you do not have any initial discussions with a potential acquirer until you are ready; otherwise, you could either lose a prospect or find yourself underselling the business even at such an early stage.

CHAPTER 8

I DON'T HAVE ENOUGH MONEY TO IMPROVE MY BUSINESS

What if you need to spend some money on your business but don't want to or can't afford to improve the business? You may have several reasons why this may be the case, but this is an important decision and one you should consider carefully. It may significantly affect the value you extract when you sell your business.

If you follow a process similar to the one I outline in Section 3, you will identify a number of areas of your business you could improve to create additional value for a prospective buyer. Some of these may require investment. The first thing to consider is whether or not you should spend the money on those projects. If you have several areas to spend money on, you need to evaluate each one both on its own merits and in comparison to the other projects because unless you have unlimited funds, it is likely you will have to prioritise the order you do them in and, indeed, if you do them at all. You may benefit from an external consultant or advisor experienced in creating additional value in a business to review your business and help you identify and build a business case for each project. You have grown the business and look at it the same way every day. It sometimes takes an outsider to review a business to see what else could be done. It is important to note that in this scenario, you are only looking to improve the business for what a prospective buyer would value and ultimately pay for. Therefore, having someone who knows how a buyer thinks and values can be instrumental in this process. Not everyone who sells businesses can do this as it requires a different skill set. I cover this in more detail in Section 3.

Once you have determined the various projects, produced business cases for each and prioritised them, you now need to decide which (if any) you should execute. There is no point in spending money on a business to improve it if it is unlikely that a potential buyer will value it enough to pay more. Assuming they would, and it makes sense to invest the money, you should review it just as you would any typical investment in your business – is there an excellent financial return for the money you would need to invest? Once you have decided it is a good business decision, you must find the most effective ways to fund it. You may then encounter a challenge: you may not immediately have the required funds to fund the investment. A professional advisor can help you explore the funding options available to you. You may not have had experience raising debt or equity for such investments and traditionally always funded them from cash flow. It can be scary if you don't know whom to talk to.

This does not mean that you should not consider it at this stage. Sometimes, a relatively small investment can make a significant difference to the value of a company. A good corporate advisor, even if they don't provide funding facilities themselves, should be able to advise you and put you in touch with the appropriate providers. You can then decide if you want to proceed or not.

If all the numbers stack up and you believe that the investment would yield the increase in value that would warrant the investment, and you still do not want to do it, you will need to accept that you are not going to realise the maximum potential value for your business.

CHAPTER 9

I DON'T HAVE ANY TIME

Yes, you do. You have 24 hours a day or 168 hours a week to spend how you choose. A business will not sell itself. How much time you spend on it will be determined by the strength of your desire to sell, your personal experience and which professional resource you engage to assist you. But you do have the time; we all do. It depends on how you decide to spend it. Just look at Sir Richard Branson, Steven Spielberg, Elon Musk or a single, working parent with three children. How do they find the time to achieve all that they do? The difference between them and most people is that they have a clear vision of what they want to achieve and ensure that their projects or plans have top priority in their busy diaries. They do their big things first.

Ask yourself, 'If I only had one month to live and I needed to sell the business to provide financial security for my family, would I do it?'. Of course you would; we all would. It just comes down to priorities. You need to put some time aside every day to sell your business. Even if you choose the most experienced and capable advisor to shoulder most of the workload, you will still need to meet with them, discuss tactics, exchange information, attend meetings with prospective buyers, etc. It isn't saleable if your business cannot operate without you for an hour a day. If a business requires its owner to be in attendance for 10 hours a day, how can they sell that to a prospective buyer?

Look at it from your prospective buyer's point of view. If you cannot spend the time required to sell your business, how will it operate once you have sold it and are no longer in it? You need to look at your work ethic from a different angle, from what you may traditionally believe is how you want to be seen. Most hard-working people want to be seen and recognised by others as someone who does just that, for working hard. They don't want people to see them having lots of holidays, taking time to attend school events or taking every Thursday afternoon off playing golf. While they may think you could have done better if you worked harder, longer, etc., prospective buyers will be pleased, as it demonstrates that you are not critical to the business. I know this cuts against the grain, and we all want to feel that we are indispensable, but a buyer does not want that at all. They want to see that the business operates daily and for short extended periods without you. How would we explain that you cannot take the time to sell your business?

This may all sound unfair; you are unlikely to have three to four hours a day spare that you can dedicate to the sales process of your business, but that is the amount of time needed when you get into the depth of the process.

There are two key ways you can create the time required, both of which should add to maximising the value of your business, so a win-win.

1. **Delegate the sale of the business process.** Appoint someone to manage and coordinate the sales process so you do not have to. This doesn't mean the coordinator has to do all the work, nor are they likely to have all the knowledge to sell your business, but the lead role is the most demanding. Ideally, you would engage a professional advisor with significant experience in selling a business and, therefore, know every element and what is required. A good idea is to supplement this with an internal resource that can collect the raw information for the advisor. This would be someone you trust and already has access to your confidential information (e.g. your accounts person). You, of course, still have to have an input into the process. You need to make critical decisions and attend specific meetings, but not everything is reliant on you; you have appointed people who will be more efficient than yourself, demonstrating to the buyer that you are comfortable delegating significant responsibilities.

2. **Delegate the running of your business.** This doesn't have to be all of the business (unless you have a number two that you believe is ready and whom you want to prepare for post-sale). Still, if you look at everything you do, there will be activities and responsibilities that others can do. So why not delegate them now? Allow your staff the opportunity to learn new things, take on added responsibility and free up some time for yourself.

Another reason you should delegate and create more time for yourself is that selling your business can take up to a year, which is a significant amount of time. While that time is elapsing, your potential acquirer will ask for updates on trading, financials and all other aspects of your business, including sales and your new business pipeline. At the very least, you must ensure that your business achieves what you predicted and shows moderate growth. But how fantastic would it be if the business beat its financial targets every month and found new revenue streams and clients? This would be an excellent use of your time. When did you last spend a couple of hours daily finding new clients? What would be the results if you did?

Most people selling their business will get distracted by the process, which can harm the business's short- and long-term performance and may lead the buyer to look for a price reduction. Be the exception; grow the value of the business so you may have the opportunity to renegotiate and increase the price. At the very least, demonstrate to the buyers that this is a better business than they first thought and that they should conclude their due diligence and complete the deal.

Make the time; it's that simple.

SECTION 3

YOUR STEPS TO SUCCESS

CHAPTER 10

THE EBITDA+™ SIX STEPS TO SUCCESS METHODOLOGY

Earlier, we discussed that while there may be twists and turns and ups and downs to navigate, selling a business will follow a particular pattern, or more accurately, several steps must be followed for a sale to occur.

However, to maximise the value of your business (e.g. engineering a $30M exit), there needs to be additional stages and actions taken. You will need to be guided by an experienced advisor who is not only competent in managing the transaction but who sees your business 'through a buyer's eyes' and guides you on how to build and execute a strategy to increase the value of your business.

As I said at the beginning, this isn't a book on how to sell your business. This book shows you how to maximise the value of your business so you get the best price possible. If you just want a quick sale and/or aren't prepared to invest time and money to improve your business, then the process following is not for you, and neither, probably, is this book.

I will take you through the six-stage process I developed for my clients through the learning I gained from over 50 transactions. Of course, there are many other approaches by very professional and competent advisors. However, I have found that by adopting this methodology and executing the actions required, I have been able to raise the value of my clients' businesses significantly, have a higher success rate of achieving a successful sale and keep them sane in the process. You will note that my process and services go beyond what a typical advisor would offer. That is because to maximise the value of a business, you first need to do a strategic review and then build and execute a plan to achieve that additional value.

Whether you adopt my process, someone else's or build your own, you should have one. There are many moving parts and things that happen simultaneously or become delayed. Ensuring you have a process and methodology to deal with those things will help you get the maximum price. This is not a time when you can make it up as you go along, even if you only want a quick sale. In particular, if you want to maximise the value of your business when it comes time to sell, then you need a process; nothing will happen by chance.

A process to maximise value differs from a process just to make a sale. It needs a minimum of the following aspects:

- Establish the current value of your business and your financial expectations from a sale. You have to establish your starting position and then know what 'success' will look like. Remember, 'begin with the end in mind'.

- Determine what the business could potentially be worth. This is much harder and is not something you can do alone.

You will need to engage an advisor or strategic consultant to help determine the very best your business could be and the maximum price a business could bring in your sector. There will be a maximum that you can achieve, and there is no point in adding value above it if your sector will not yield that value. For example, while a traditional manufacturing sector may have a value multiple between 3–6 × EBITDA, an IT or technology business could work off multiples in the 9–12 × EBITDA. In a fast-growing sector like AI or SaaS, you would be working with multiples of revenue, not EBITDA. So, a manufacturing business cannot achieve the same multiple values as an IT business.

- Build a plan to realise the potential value.
- Have a solid methodology/process/resource to execute the plan.

After all of the above is completed, or at least well on track, the sales process can start with its own rhythm and process.

The EBITDA+™ SIX STEPS TO SUCCESS methodology

The definition of EBITDA in financial terminology is earnings before interest, tax, depreciation and amortisation. It is viewed by many as a reliable view of a company's financial cash performance.

I have adapted it to describe the six-stage process I use, which is entirely appropriate in a business sale, as one of the most common valuation methodologies used for buying and selling businesses is EBITDA × a multiple (a coefficient). In Australia, over 70% of businesses are valued and acquired this way.

EBITDA+™ SIX STEPS TO SUCCESS in my context stands for:

- **Evaluate** the Gap
- **Bridge** the Gap
- **Information**
- **The Deal**
- **Due diligence**
- **After the event**

The following chapters will take you through the details of what each entails and the reason for adopting it.

CHAPTER 11

EVALUATE THE GAP

'Begin with the end in mind' is a well-known habit in Steven Covey's *The seven habits of highly effective people*. Put simply, before starting on a journey, you need to know where you are going; otherwise, how will you know that you have arrived, or, indeed, how will you know what success looks like? Likewise, selling a business for the 'right price' must be worked out before starting any process, not just as a knee-jerk reaction to an offer a prospective buyer submits.

Of course, there are numerous valuations a business could have at any time. Still, there are always at least three that should be considered:

1. **What it is 'technically' worth.** This valuation is provided by a valuation expert, an experienced advisor or an accountant. As we have already seen, there are numerous ways in which it can be calculated. Note that it is not just a financial calculation. A good valuation methodology will consider several non-financial elements of the business and

its financial performance. Given the number of valuation methodologies, the most appropriate one must be used for the business. The other non-financial elements are critical to define because the hidden value (or ability to maximise a valuation) often sits within these elements. I have described some of these in the following chapter.

2. **What a current owner believes it is worth (or the amount they want to sell it for).** This is often also confused with what an owner needs from the sale (covered in chapter 6). This should be what an owner believes their business is worth based on their knowledge and experience within their industry sector and their detailed business knowledge. Inevitably, and perhaps predictably, most owners are very optimistic about what their business is worth. They often place a higher value than a buyer or an independent valuer would. It is good for a business owner to glean as much market intelligence on what other similar businesses to theirs have been sold for, even if they have engaged a professional advisor. The seller will always know the industry better than someone outside the sector. Trade magazines, discussions with other owners in their field, etc., are ways to find useful information.

3. **What a potential buyer believes it is worth.** Putting aside what negotiating tactics a prospective buyer may adopt (e.g. a low initial offer), this is the amount that a potential buyer genuinely believes the business is worth and what they would be prepared to pay for it. This is not always as obvious to the seller as you might think because it goes beyond what we know about their business. For example, you may have some key clients that the buyer has wanted to gain for their

business, not just to sell products or services you supply but ones you don't. They may save significant back-office costs by merging the two businesses, even relocating one of them. Sometimes, a buyer may surprise a seller because they are prepared to pay a higher price to gain those hidden benefits, particularly if they believe someone else is interested in your business. Like in many aspects of business, knowing your competitor's business (or, in this case, your buyer) may give you a competitive advantage.

What really matters at this stage are two sets of numbers:

1. What a professional valuer, advisor or accountant values the business to be worth;
2. What an owner wants/needs from the sale of the business.

The difference between these two numbers can be defined as 'the gap'. Once we know this number, we move on to the next stage, 'Bridge the Gap'. Before we do, I want to explore what goes into and influences the 'multiple' part of a multiple valuation, given that it is the most common method used in Australia. It is also a critical and often overlooked (by sellers) part of the valuation. If you remember the example in Chapter 3, we used a business producing $5M EBITDA, and the industry multiple was 3–5 × EBITDA. As we saw, this would deliver a valuation range of between $15M and $25M, which is a very significant variation. The only part that changed was the multiple coefficients we used. The profit or EBITDA, in this case, remained the same. So, what makes the difference, and how can you create a business at the high end of the multiple range rather than at the lower?

In Chapter 2, I used an iceberg analogy to illustrate that the negotiation is just the tip of what constitutes the price a business may attract and that the real value is below the water line. I will now expand on some of those items and pose critical questions to ensure a 'good score' for some key areas and also what will bring them down.

Financial strength/quality of earnings

A business purchaser is fundamentally acquiring future cash flows. Hence, a business's financial strength and quality of earnings are critical. The following points/questions are examples of the types of items that need to be considered:

1. **Profit and loss statement** – What is the company's record of financial performance? Has it had revenue growth, increased profits, solid cost management and consistent margins?

2. **Balance sheet** – While the balance sheet (depending on the valuation method) might not form part of the immediate calculation, a savvy and financially literate buyer will review the balance sheet in detail as it will tell them a lot about the financial health of the business and the way it has been managed. A strong, clean, healthy balance sheet can significantly affect how a buyer views a business and how the owner has been managing it.

3. **Margin** – What are the current and historical margins for the business? Have they been growing or declining? How do they compare with industry norms?

4. **Bank ratios/covenants** – Have they been breached? Has the company operated within any banking covenants? What do they look like they will do in the next 12 months?

5. **Budgeting/forecasting achievement** – Has the company had a solid budget setting and re-forecasting process? If so, how have they fared? Do they hit or beat their initial budget, or are they always re-forecasting down and missing the revised forecasts?

6. **Financial reporting/literacy** – What reports are available? What financial software and reporting package do they use? Are they detailed and insightful, or do they just use a bookkeeper and only produce the statutory minimum once a year? Have they a CFO, or do they use an external CFO service or none at all?

7. **Statutory payments** – Are superannuation and tax payments up to date? Do they pay them in line with best practice, or have they had a history of being late and being on a payment plan?

8. **Wage bill** – What are the amounts of annual leave and long service leave? Have they been well managed, or are they a significant liability that the buyer must assume?

Market attractiveness

How attractive is the market sector the company operates in? Is it a growing sector or a declining one? Will it benefit from digitalisation and globalisation, or could the entire sector disappear? Are there adjacent markets that the company could evolve into over time? What opportunities are there in the sector for further acquisitions? If the company only currently sells to an Australian customer base, are there opportunities overseas in the same sector? What are the barriers to entry for the sector or can anyone become a competitor operating from a bedroom with a laptop?

A potential acquirer will probably know your sector well. If they knocked on your door, they were likely interested in your sector before they got there.

Company attractiveness

How attractive is a company to a buyer? This is a difficult question as there are many buyer types. They will all be looking for some specific/unique attributes. Regardless, there are some common items we need to be aware of when looking at a business through the eyes of a potential buyer:

1. **Ease of running the business** – Can it be taught to someone who has never worked in this sector? Can the next level of managers reporting to the owners manage the day-to-day operation by reporting to a country manager or even an overseas manager?

2. **Capital expenditure** – Are there significant annual capital expenditure requirements? If a business has high equipment levels, what condition are they in? Are any about to become obsolete, and may the buyer face extensive replacement or upkeep costs?

3. **Labour relations (e.g. unions, employee agreements)** – What are industrial relations like between management and employees? What formal agreements are in place? How might they affect a potential acquirer's business if they were to acquire your business and merge them?

4. **Building lease obligations** – How long is left on the building leases? What could the make-good costs be? How difficult/costly would it be to terminate a lease early?

5. **Ease of integration** – How easy is it for the company to be relocated? Is the workforce mobile and more likely to be open to a new location, or do most catch public transport and are less flexible to a significant change?

6. **Room for growth** – Could the buyer fit more people, equipment, etc., into the current facility? This could be positive if the building has a long lease (which can also be seen as a negative) and if the business has room for growth or to merge another business into the same footprint.

Competitive advantage

Has the company got significant competitors in its sector? Is it seen as a leader? Have they developed processes, systems, products and services that others struggle to copy? How do they win? Is it sustainable or under threat? What could threaten their competitive advantage? Have they leveraged it to the maximum, or are there additional opportunities? How does the company's financials compare against its competitors? Does it have the balance sheet strength to do things that the less-resourced competitors cannot?

Revenue profile

A revenue profile is different from client revenue. What you need to be able to present here is in what form you obtain your revenue. What level of detail can you report on? How often is the information collected? What is the review process of the revenue structure? What is the structure of your revenue? In a service business, how much is recurring or one-off project-based?

How is it captured/managed? What channels are there? Have you an online business? Do you have a sales force on the road? Do you sell on price or service? Is it retained, project-based or product-based?

Client profile

Regardless of the type of business, e.g. asset-heavy or service, I cannot stress enough the importance of your clients and how well they are protected for a buyer. The buyer needs confidence that all or most of your top 10 clients will transfer through a change of ownership at the end of the due diligence period. If they maintain the current levels of quality, service, pricing, etc., do they have a good chance of retaining and growing your clients? What is the profile of the client base? How many clients does the business have? What proportion of revenue do the top 10 clients make up? The top five? How long has the business had its clients? How many of them are contracted? How hard is it to service them? Are any under threat? Would any of them leave if there was a change of ownership? Does the client have the right to terminate the contract or renegotiate the terms under a change of ownership?

Business development

What is the company's approach to business development, or does it rely on its current clients, repeat business and referrals? Has it a clear strategy for growth? What role does the business owner play? Is there dedicated business development staff, or is it ad hoc and just fitted in?

IT systems and business processes

Has the business the necessary hardware and software to operate effectively today? Will they be able to cope with significant growth? How difficult are they to integrate into another company's software and systems? Is it well known and off the shelf, or developed by an individual without backup? How secure is the data? What are their IT policies? Have they a disaster recovery plan? How realistic is it?

Intellectual property (IP)

If a business has some IP, is registered and protected, and provides a competitive commercial advantage, it can be like gold. It is a complicated area, and dangerous to talk generically about it. Still, true IP can significantly raise the value of a business, particularly if:

- the current owners haven't fully exploited it
- it hasn't been taken to all available markets
- it could be used in the buyer's own business
- it could be developed and sold off in its own right in the future
- it is well protected.

Marketing and promotion

Does the business have a marketing plan? Does it have dedicated marketing and promotions staff? How does it attract new business in its sector? Is it known as a leader? If so, how does the business ensure it is kept front of mind? Does the business write/ publish papers? What is the quality of its website? Does anyone from the business speak at conferences? Do they attend exhibitions, trade shows, etc.?

People – risk profile

People and their effectiveness are one of the most critical success aspects of any business and one of the hardest to conduct due diligence on for a buyer. The following questions relate to the people involved in the business and the risk profile they create and form some of the questions a buyer will want answered.

1. **Owner dependency.** How dependent on the owners is the business? How many holidays does the owner take? What is their management structure? What levels of accountability do the direct reports to the owners have? What training and personal development do they have?

2. **Key staff.** How many staff report to the owners? What skills and experiences do they have? How long have they been in the business? Have they worked anywhere else before? Can any of them step into the owner's shoes? What is the labour turnover of the key staff? When and whom was the last key person who left? Why did they leave?

3. **HR policies and structure.** Is there a formal HR structure to ensure the wellbeing and professional management of the employees?

4. **Workplace health and safety (WHS) management.** How well has WHS been led and managed? Does the business take it seriously, or are there big cultural issues for a prospective buyer?

Business maturity

Does the business have a long-term strategic plan? If so, what is it planning to do? What evidence is there of them successfully executing a long-term plan? Who created the plan? Did they engage an outside facilitator? Who was involved in building the plan, or was it just the owners? Does the business have a formal board? Does it have an advisory committee? Does the business undertake any market analysis? Does anyone in the business travel to find new ideas? If so, what success have they had?

Be game ready

The above questions are not extensive by any means. I could write pages of questions I would ask when evaluating a business, all of which I would factor into a valuation. Other areas may be critical in some industries more than others (e.g. ESG – environmental, social, governance). In some of these areas, great value can be gained or lost.

Not every buyer would ask all of these questions. You might get lucky; they may not dig deep or widely enough, but if your business is not in top shape across a wide range of areas, and if you come across a sophisticated and experienced buyer, expect them to uncover all your weak spots. On a positive note, if your business is in tip-top shape, not only can you demand the high end of the multiple range, but you will have a very excited and committed buyer who should be moving very quickly to acquire you with minimal conditions. It's a bit like being fit and prepared enough to enter the Olympics compared to some who might go to the gym just a few times a week. Consider all the aspects a top athlete has to get right – diet, exercise, clothing, sleep, mental state, hours of training, etc. Compare that with someone who is relatively fit and healthy; you need to be the top athlete prepared for the Olympics to get the maximum price possible. You need to be 'game ready'. This is what we are here for. This is what this book is all about.

CHAPTER 12

BRIDGE THE GAP

Once you have evaluated a business, produced a financial value and understand the owner's financial requirement from the sale, you can establish if there is a difference between the two numbers. Several scenarios could eventuate from this exercise:

- The owner's requirement is less than the value of their business, and the sale is likely to deliver a higher price than the owner requires. In my experience, this is rare! It is not very often that an owner will value their business or want less from a sale than what it is truly worth.

- The owner's requirement is the same as what it is worth. Again rare, as per the above.

- The owner's requirement is more than what it is worth. Sadly, this is the most common. While an owner knows their business better than anyone else, they may not always see its weaknesses. They may also have an overinflated view of what a prospective purchaser will pay for their business.

Regardless of the above, the valuation process will have high-lighted several opportunities to increase the value of the business. This is what 'Engineering a $30M Exit' is all about. An owner may be satisfied with their business delivering the financial outcome they originally sought; however, they should want to get the maximum value (create life-changing wealth). To do so, they must build and execute a plan ahead of the sales process. There are also a couple of additional reasons why a business owner should explore all opportunities to increase the value of their business further.

If, in theory, the business is worth what the owner wants or needs, it is just a theoretical valuation at this stage, and a buyer prepared to pay that value still has to be found. Therefore, it is important to increase the value of the business higher than what an owner wants to allow some wriggle room in the negotiation process, which can be used to the owner's advantage. For example, they could:

- negotiate a quick transaction in exchange for a reduced price
- have some wriggle room in case a prospective buyer finds something meaningful in due diligence
- be able to negotiate a swifter transition period for a reduction in price
- pocket a higher price.

So, the gap has now been established. Either a gap between what an owner requires from the sale of their business or between the true potential of the business and what it is worth now and/or what an owner requires.

I will not proceed beyond this stage with a client until we have thoroughly analysed these valuation scenarios and agreed to the 'numbers'. If we don't complete this process correctly, how will we know if we have succeeded?

Remember, 'begin with the end in mind'.

So, why do so few providers follow this approach, and what is the process to build and execute a plan?

- **Time.** Some owners do not want to spend 12 months + preparing their business for sale. Also, many advisors, brokers and agents will not risk working with a client for this length of time. Their business model is based on executing a transaction as quickly as possible.

- **The capability of the advisor, broker or agent.** To fully evaluate a business (as I have described) and execute a business improvement plan requires the capability and experience that not all providers have. This does not mean they are incapable of selling a business. However, if they haven't bought many businesses (and can't think like a buyer) or created (and delivered) long-term strategic plans for a business, they will not have the capability or experience to provide this service effectively.

- **The cost structure of the provider.** As you would expect, large accounting firms, corporate advisors and banking organisations may have teams with the capability and experience to build and deliver such an approach. The reason small firms don't is one of cost and capability. Their cost structure and business model would not accommodate a process that sometimes could take a couple of years.

A high-level view of the process I follow once we have established the gap is:

- **Setting up an advisory committee.** An advisory committee does not have the same responsibilities or authority as a corporate board, nor are its participants necessarily directors (though some individuals might be, e.g. the owners). It will solely focus on increasing the value and the successful sale of the business. As a result, they will not be distracted by the business's day-to-day operations or regulatory requirements, which is the role and responsibility of the company's management and directors. The committee would meet regularly to monitor the performance of the management team in delivering the strategic plan.

- **Building a strategic plan.** Every aspect that constitutes value in a business must be addressed, and a plan put in place for each aspect to maximise the value of the business. If executed properly, this detailed plan will increase the value of the business in the eyes of a buyer.

- **Resourcing the plan/allocating responsibilities.** This includes who within the advisory committee and management team has to deliver what actions, but it may also include investment that needs to be made in the business.

- **Roll-up-sleeve action sessions.** Led by my team, these action working sessions are where we work on a specific part of the business or plan that may need special attention, focus or experience. Although these sessions can be wide-ranging and challenging, they certainly are not talkfests. They are often used when something has gone off track or has changed in the external environment, and remedial action needs to be taken.

The plan

The strategic plan is critical as it evaluates not only areas within the company that can be improved but also in the context of what is happening in the external world and the company's sector, not just their immediate competitors.

There are many ways to build a strategic plan; different business consultants use various well-known methodologies or have developed their own. While any well-run strategic planning process will produce a benefit and should increase the value of a business, the difference in this approach is that it is done with a very clear focus on who the plan is for, i.e. the prospective buyer. When I run a strategic review of a business, I build a plan of the priorities that need to be addressed through a buyer's eyes and not through the eyes of a seller. This is a critical point. For your plan to truly maximise the value when you come to sell it, it must deliver what a buyer will value and pay for. Here are a few key points to remember when doing a strategic review:

1. Strategy is about deciding what you will do and, just as importantly, what you will not do. No business (in any circumstance) can do everything possible simultaneously. Apart from the monetary investment, the organisation and its people would be unable to cope. So, you have to make some choices and focus on strategies that will deliver the most value (through a buyer's eyes).

2. You need to collect intelligence about your business and the external market; otherwise, you will not be informed and may miss the bigger picture.

3. A well-executed strategic plan will significantly increase your chances of success but will not guarantee it. Despite all the

best intentions and being as informed as possible, events out of our control (e.g. a natural disaster) can appear from nowhere and spoil the best-laid plans. This does not mean, however, that you should not make one. It will significantly increase the odds of your success.

4. It isn't easy. It requires discipline, stretching your mind and looking at things you may have done before or even discarded. If it didn't require hard work or focus and 'just happened', everyone would be doing it, and you would have no competitive advantage. You must keep thinking of the prize; you want to create life-changing wealth for yourself and your family.

I use various strategic models and processes depending on my client's business sector and what I feel will work best for the owners and their management teams. Regarding management teams, I like to build the strategic plan with more input than just the owners. If possible, getting the team's input is critical. In all cases, the owners and key employees know most of what is needed. A process should be designed to ensure that all available knowledge, experience and capability are included in the model and that nothing is missed. It always delights me to see at the end of the first stage of running a strategy review how much the team in the business knows. They always come up with far more solutions and things they can do to increase the value of the business than they can execute, which is just what is needed.

The plan, as well as identifying the things the business is going to do, will assign very specific responsibilities and deadlines. This is critical; otherwise, it just becomes a pretty document that sits in a desk drawer at risk of not being actioned.

Once the advisory committee has signed off on the plan, they will monitor the achievement of the plan at regular intervals and step in when required to get it back on track. Having a body accountable (ideally detached from the day-to-day running of the business) for the overall achievement of the plan is important. Without accountability and responsibility for the overall plan, it gets left to the individuals, and not all aspects will be delivered. You have to understand the importance of making this plan happen. It is the blueprint to increase the value of the business and, therefore, must become the owner's top priority. It will also give a buyer confidence that the business is well disciplined and has an approach and methodology to achieve strategic growth.

Please note that every business is different, as are every owner's circumstances, so while there is a pattern/approach I follow, it is always tailored to each unique situation.

CHAPTER 13

INFORMATION (PREPARATION) AND DISSEMINATION

Information and dissemination are other areas of a sales process where an owner asks, 'Where do I start?'. There are two fundamental ways to provide potential buyers with information about your business.

1. You (or your advisor) prepare a fully comprehensive, detailed set of information to professionally demonstrate all aspects of the business.

2. You wait for a prospective buyer to tell you what they need to know.

There are three reasons why I would strongly advise you to take the initiative and make the time and effort to prepare the information thoroughly before being asked.

1. It significantly reduces the time taken for this part of the process.

2. It lets you control this critical (in value) part of the process. You want to ensure that you present the items of significant value to a buyer in a way that represents them best.

3. You will appear much more professional to the potential buyer. Remember, part of the value they are prepared to pay for your business is their perception of how well it is run.

Again, doing this to the very highest standard takes time, as there will be missing elements, some of which need to be started from scratch, so the earlier this process can start, the better. It is a good idea to start building this information right from when you/your advisor conducts the initial evaluation of the business, and just like the strategy, a detailed plan to collect the information and build the data room is required.

Now we have established it is the seller's job to provide the information, what do you have to provide? While some key items must be included, some should be presented in a particular way, depending on the strengths and weaknesses of the business. In addition, a good advisor will conduct research on the likely potential buyers, think through what synergies there may be within their business and make sure the information that shows value for them is easy to find.

I have detailed below a typical set of initial information to be provided. However, it is crucial that you do not provide all the details of your business at this stage because you have not yet received an acceptable NBIO, nor do you know if they are serious or just curious. Some people who may look at your business could well be competitors, so you have to be very careful about what information you deliver and at what point. Some information to not provide at this stage are customer or employee details, detailed market intelligence or strategic plans. However, you will still start preparing these pieces of information, as they will be needed once you have accepted an NBIO for detailed due diligence.

Key initial information includes:

1. **Financials.** You must prepare at least the last three years' profit and loss accounts in as much detail as you have. This is critical information for a buyer to make an NBIO. A buyer will also probably ask for the balance sheets for the same period. They are not necessarily needed at this stage for some types of acquisition (e.g. an asset purchase), though they will be in due diligence, and should not be provided automatically. Having said that, some buyers may insist on seeing a balance sheet, even at the earliest stage, particularly if they are acquiring the business through a share purchase. You must be prepared to provide them with it if you want to keep them in the process. Several factors must be considered, and you or your advisor must consider your response to such a request. In addition, you should have prepared your budget for the current year, your performance against that budget and any re-forecasts you have completed.

2. **Corporate structure.** You must clearly define and list the business's corporate structure, what it trades under, etc. For example, is it a Pty operated by a family trust, a partnership or shareholding?

3. **Revenue.** Annual revenues for the last three years by type/channel and client (not named; blind listing is fine at this stage) and gross margins by the same split. The buyer must have enough information to assess the structure (and risk) of your revenues, profitability and client base. At this stage, you are not to reveal any client identities; they may be a competitor, and this can wait until due diligence.

4. **Sales pipeline.** A buyer of your business wants to buy future revenue. While historical revenue and contracted clients indicate solid future revenue, they will also want to see a healthy, detailed and 'real' pipeline of future opportunities. Any healthy business should have an active and scientific process for identifying, measuring and actioning new business opportunities. Again, this should be a blind list at this stage.

5. **'Job' details.** They will want information for the last three years, depending on your business/type of products or services. This will include things like average dollar values of jobs per month, the number of jobs per month and the number of active clients per month.

6. **Top 10 client details (blind listing).** In addition to what you provided under revenue, you will need to give more detail on your top 10 clients. However, you still do not disclose the individual names of those clients. What they will probably want to see for the last three years are:

   a. each client's revenue further split into different products or services that you provide to each client

   b. the contract terms (if they are contracted)

   c. the length of time they have been a client

   d. any key or unusual commercial/payment terms

   e. any key customers lost in the last 12 months, and why

   f. general commentary on the outlook for the top 10 clients

   g. an aged debtors' ledger (again blind, not identified by name) as at year-end for the last three years.

7. **The commercial details regarding key suppliers (blind listing).**

8. **Details of key information technology systems** (detailed information regarding IT can come in due diligence).

9. **The properties and key assets.**

10. **The people:**

   a. an organisation chart (de-identified), including the number of staff by type and location

   b. the key staff (no names, just roles and length of time on the job)

   c. the owners (overview of what roles/functions they carry out).

Every potential buyer will have their own list of what they want, and not all aspects of their information request will be equal. It is a delicate balance between providing them with enough information to have adequately evaluated the value of the business to produce a realistic NBIO and giving too much information to someone who may not submit an offer. This is also a critical time in building a relationship with the potential future owner of your business. Therefore, how both parties work together on providing and reviewing the initial information is an essential foundation for future discussions. Getting this right is critical in getting a strong NBIO from a potential acquirer.

Construction of a data room

A comprehensive data room will allow potential buyers to review the company's corporate structure, operations and financial documentation. There are multiple electronic data room providers available, many good.

Most data room providers will allow you to give selected parties access to different folders and files and restrict the ability to download specific files. It may also be important to choose a platform where registered users cannot see who else has been granted access.

For most transactions, I recommend using one of the pricier data room solutions to demonstrate the seriousness and professional approach to the deal. You want to get this stage of the transaction right and move through the due diligence process as efficiently as possible. The well-established data room providers, such as Ansarada or Datasite, will allow you to track who is looking at what files, for how long and how often. This can give you a good indication of how interested a party is in pursuing a relationship. In addition, all communication can be handled within the system, keeping a record of your dialogue, minimising miscommunication and capturing what has been disclosed (very important regarding warranties).

The other important point is to have a cohesive folder structure to simplify the due diligence process. You and the potential buyer of your business will have to collect a vast number of documents and paperwork. Authorised users of your data room will need to be able to find relevant information quickly. You don't want a potential buyer to pull out of the process because it all seems too hard. The good news is that most data rooms will automatically index your information for you.

Here's an example of a basic data room folder structure:

1. Corporate
2. Contracts

3. Employees
4. Financials
5. Insurance
6. IP
7. Litigation
8. Operations
9. Properties
10. Supplier agreements
11. Tax.

Marketing the business

Part of preparing the business for sale and what information to prepare depends on how you plan to market and attract potential buyers. How do you ensure you speak to the businesses and individuals likely to be interested and see the value you have built in your business? This will have been a significant part of the strategic planning process. There should be no fixed approach; different businesses need different strategies. Most transaction providers will have a set process that includes producing an initial flyer and a more detailed information memorandum and work based on mass mailouts and following up leads. In my experience, this does not produce the best result. If your strategy is to maximise what someone will pay for your business, then part of that is precisely targeting potential buyers. That being the case, having a flyer or an information memorandum may or may not be appropriate. It needs to be determined as part of the plan. In any event, if you follow the process I highlighted earlier, you will have been collecting the relevant information, and it can be quickly collated and presented in a way the buyer requires.

The other aspect to consider if you do decide to do a generic mass market mailout of your business is that regardless of how you try and disguise the identity of your business, there is a real risk that your employees, clients or suppliers will find out you are looking to sell at a very early stage in the process, which could give you significant issues. Remember, selling a business can take much longer than you initially think. It is common for a business to go through an extended process with a potential buyer for several months, only for the intended sale to fall over at the last minute. Did you really want your critical stakeholders distracted and unsettled in this situation? What will you say to them when you haven't sold and have to start again?

This is a particular and tailored part of the plan. I will not detail a generic approach in this book, as I don't follow one or recommend it. For example, I once identified two businesses that should both be very interested and had the resources to pay for a client's business. I discretely approached both parties and spoke to them about an anonymous business with high-level information on key metrics to gauge interest. After both expressed their strong interest, I ran a process with only those two businesses involved until they both submitted an NBIO. We then granted exclusivity to one of the parties after accepting their NBIO, with a time constraint as to how long they had to complete their due diligence and the deal. This worked exceptionally well, and the first time the employees, customers and suppliers knew there was a change of ownership was after the deal was complete and the money was in the bank. I have had another client for whom we decided to run an international process, which had to be far more research-based with a higher number of potential buyers we had to reach. In this example, we did produce an initial (anonymous) flyer, followed by a detailed information memorandum once we had qualified a party's interest. We ran a process for four interested parties in three countries for most of the initial two stages to maintain competitive tension. This enabled us to maximise the value we attained and provided a safety net in case the preferred buyer dropped out. In this situation, we also had to advise the employees earlier in the process that the owner was looking to transition the business to a new owner safely. However, running an open and regular communication process with them avoided any significant issues for the business or its people.

CHAPTER 14

THE DEAL

Following my comments regarding how to market (or not) your business, it is essential to know your prospective buyers. For a buyer to pay the maximum for your business, having it in as good a shape as possible is not enough, though that is obviously important. You have to solve a problem or create a unique opportunity for a potential buyer to get their maximum interest. You need to give them additional value to their business over and above just adding your revenues and profits. To ensure you have the best chance of doing this, it then follows that you need to know as much as you can about your potential buyers. The sooner you build your intelligence and the more detailed it is, the sooner you can work on your business to provide the added value that will get them to pay the top price. Simple!

Suppose you have done your homework, have potential buyers in a process and have one (or ideally more than one) who wants to proceed to the next stage (which I have named 'the Deal'): the negotiation. At this stage, you will have provided the buyer with enough information and answered any subsequent questions to determine if they want to submit an offer and the value (and any required conditions) they are prepared to put forward. Note they haven't done due diligence yet, and you have not provided them with the level of detail they need to be legally bound by their offer. So, what they will be submitting is a Non-Binding Indicative Offer (NBIO).

An NBIO will have both the financial value a buyer is prepared to pay and any key terms or conditions they require as part of their financial offer. An example of a condition could be requiring the owner to continue to work in the business for some time after completion to ensure the safe transition of the client base.

While not legally binding, an NBIO should be taken very seriously. Both parties should do everything possible to ensure it represents the final purchase price, structure and conditions. If the initial information provided was accurate and the subsequent questions were professionally answered, the price detailed in an NBIO should not change through the due diligence process. This is the time to push hard for both the value and structure of the deal. It is better to discover at this stage any conditions, terms or potential issues that may be part of a final offer rather than later in the process.

How should you best manage the actual negotiation itself? Some business owners will be strong negotiators, while others will not. I firmly believe that in both cases, it gives an advantage to a seller if they engage a professional advisor to lead the negotiations on their behalf. The reason is evident for owners who are not comfortable or are not strong negotiators. It is such a critical stage in maximising the value, and you only get one shot at it. If an owner agrees to a price in an NBIO, they cannot negotiate a higher price later on unless an exceptional event occurs (such as a major contract win). An owner who is a strong negotiator will still be in a stronger position if they engage a professional on their behalf, as it allows them to participate in the negotiation at strategic points. They and the advisor can play 'good cop/bad cop' if required. In both cases, selling a business is an emotional time for any owner. The negotiation element, particularly when faced with a buyer trying to find flaws and minimise the price they pay, can be very upsetting, and emotion can get in the way of negotiating the best price.

So, what does a good negotiation process look like? I often get asked what tricks, skills and processes the best negotiators follow. What tips can I pass on? I do not believe it is that simple. Sure, if it is a straightforward, quick sale, the primary (sometimes only) tool in a negotiator's toolbox is their individual skill instead of the buyer's.

If you reflect on what we have discussed in the book so far, and if a business has been as well prepared as I am suggesting it needs to be, the negotiation is the end of a buyer valuing a business, not the main event. I try not to get into a face-to-face negotiation with a potential buyer unless I am pretty sure I know what they are likely to offer. That can only be done by all the hard work beforehand. I am not saying that negotiation meetings and face-to-face 'bartering' are not part of the process, merely that it is not the main event if there has been a good process and value created in the run-up to the negotiation.

Once the negotiations are complete and there is an agreed purchase price and key conditions, both parties sign the NBIO. This important document should be as detailed as possible as it will form the commercial basis for the sale and purchase agreement the lawyers will draw up. While the NBIO must accurately portray the offer, it is not a long document (two to six pages). It is typically drawn up by the buyer (or their advisor), not a lawyer.

While discussing the NBIO, we should speak of exclusivity for a prospective buyer. Most, if not all, potential buyers will, at some stage, ask for exclusivity in the sales process of your business. They ask that while they are still in discussions with you, they are the only party with access to your information and that you only hold any discussions with them. This is not an unreasonable request from them. They will be spending significant time, money and staffing resources reviewing your business. The last thing they need is to get to the end of the process, and at the 11th hour, you decide to sell to another party. However, from a seller's perspective, you do not want to have only one potential buyer too early in the process. A workable compromise is agreeing to a defined time for exclusivity with clearly defined stages (following the execution of an acceptable NBIO).

CHAPTER 15
DUE DILIGENCE

Immediately following the signing of the NBIO, the parties move into due diligence. The due diligence process is there for the buyer to check and test the business to be satisfied that it is worth the price they offered in the NBIO.

At this stage, the owner needs to disclose significant additional information as requested by the buyer. Most buyers will ask for everything to be fully disclosed, e.g. client and employee names, future sales pipelines, etc. Though most sellers will automatically provide them, believing they have no option, this is not the case. Some information considered sensitive (covered by privacy laws) can be held back, i.e. in a 'black box', undisclosed until just before the signing of the sale and purchase agreement. There is even an option for some information only to be provided after signing the sale and purchase agreement as a condition precedent (CP) to completion.

How exhaustive and detailed due diligence is depends on several factors, including:

- the capability of the buyer
- if there are specialist 'due diligence' parties engaged (e.g. corporate advisors)
- the professionalism and completeness of the initial information provided
- the number and size of any discrepancies found compared with what was disclosed in the initial information process
- the agreed price of the business
- the complexity, geographical locations and size of the business
- any unique aspects, e.g. specialised systems, IP
- the type of purchase. If it is a simple asset sale, the amount of due diligence required is significantly less than a complicated share sale
- the keenness of the buyer to acquire the business
- if there is any competitive tension, i.e. another party is in discussions.

To understand the level of detail that may be required, I have provided a summary of what a typical legal due diligence request may look like (from Hitch Advisory, Sydney). Please note that this is a starting point only. Request lists will vary based on various factors, including if it is an asset or share sale purchase and the type of business being reviewed. The other aspect is that once you have provided the information, you will be asked numerous follow-up questions, which will be very specific and in areas they either do not understand, have concerns about or see a potential upside. So, while a buyer may follow a generic list like the one that follows or has developed their own, it will be altered and influenced by your business type and what was discovered in the initial information stage. Each sub-section below will be further broken down into several more sections.

1. The Business
   1.1 Background
   1.2 Material transactions
   1.3 Management structure

2. Corporate
   2.1 Capital structure
   2.2 Security interests over shares, etc.
   2.3 Agreements affecting share capital or control
   2.4 Statutory registers
   2.5 Constitution
   2.6 Share and option plans

3. Related Party and Non-Arm's-Length Transactions
   3.1 Related party transactions
   3.2 Non-arm's-length transactions

4. Assets
   4.1 Relevant assets
   4.2 Security interests over assets, etc.
   4.3 Assets outside Australia
   4.4 Assets to be included in the proposed transaction

5. Finance
   5.1 Borrowings
   5.2 Loans
   5.3 Security documents
   5.4 Equipment and finance leases, hire purchase agreements, etc.

11. Information Technology
    11.1 IT systems
    11.2 Storage and access of data
    11.3 Shared access
    11.4 IT policies
    11.5 Disputes
    11.6 Hardware and equipment
    11.7 Websites
    11.8 Source code
    11.9 Insurance
    11.10 IT agreements

12. Employees
    12.1 Schedule of employees
    12.2 Consultants and independent contractors
    12.3 Directors and senior management
    12.4 Awards cover
    12.5 Claims by employees

13. Superannuation
    13.1 Details of funds
    13.2 No defined benefits
    13.3 No superannuation guarantee charge

14. Privacy
    14.1 Personal information

15. Insurance
    15.1 Current and historic claims

16. Stamp Duty
    16.1 Status of stamp duty

17. Attorneys and Representatives
    17.1 Agency
    17.2 Attorney

17.3   Commissions

18. Other Material Information

18.1   General

Source: Hitch Advisory Pty Ltd

Disclaimer: This document must be used with care and modified to reflect the particular circumstances in which it is proposed. No person should rely on this document without first obtaining legal advice from a qualified lawyer and reviewing the document to ascertain if it is appropriate for the intended use. This document does not comprise legal, accounting or other professional advice. Hitch Advisory Pty Ltd does not warrant that this document is fit for any specific purpose, including without limitation compliance with any legal requirements that may be applicable to you.

As you can see from the above, the amount and level of detail required in a due diligence process is significantly more than in the initial information phase. There may also be a separate request specific to tax and accounting due diligence, which accountants usually conduct. It is critical in this stage not to take the questions personally or get upset if a buyer challenges you and your business on key facts or assumptions. They must be sure that what you represented in the initial information stage, in which they subsequently made an offer, was accurate and a true representation of the business.

While it may be a painful process at times, it is far better for both parties to be satisfied with the commercial and operating elements of the deal and the relationship between buyer and seller, particularly if there is a requirement for the owner to work in the business post-sale.

Managing a due diligence process itself is a skill. It needs a very disciplined approach to ensure that all the information is presented professionally and all questions are collected and responded to in a complete and timely manner. The quality and accuracy of these responses are also critical, as the buyer is valuing the business based on their own analysis of the information you provide.

Due diligence also marks the introduction of each party's legal team/lawyer in two key aspects:

1. The creation and execution of the sale and purchase agreement (also known as a business sale agreement)
2. The leading of legal due diligence.

This book does not intend to cover the legal process in any detail. It would be a book on its own. All that is covered here is the advisor's role in the legal process and where they add value.

Managing the legal process/the business sale agreement

This is a critical area where an experienced and skilful negotiator/advisor can add real value to the sales process. Many people believe that managing the creation and execution of the legals is just left to the lawyers. However, a good advisor can add significant value and support to the lawyers and the process. In every sale and purchase agreement, there are two key elements:

1. The legal aspects
2. The commercial aspects.

These areas need direction and leadership from both the buyer and seller (or their representatives). The commercial aspect is relatively easy to understand. As the process goes through its many twists and turns, each party will need to give some ground to adjust the agreement so that it is fair and representative of issues as they unfold. A lawyer will not typically make a commercial judgement; it is not their remit, nor do they have the in-depth knowledge of the business financials or operations to make such an informed decision. If the lawyers can't do it, why not the owner and buyer? In short, they can, but understanding the commercial issue needs negotiating and translating back to the lawyers. This isn't easy to do if you don't have significant experience reviewing legal documents, discussing and negotiating a commercial aspect and communicating it back to the lawyers.

What about the legal aspects? Obviously, the lawyers are the experts here. Unless you are a qualified lawyer, you can't and shouldn't try to detail the points of the legal documents (they won't let you anyway). However, even the legal aspects have an element of 'commercialisation' or 'risk' positioning. It may well be that a lawyer is technically correct on an issue. Still, an owner is prepared to take a risk on it – warranties are a good example here. Warranties form part of the sale agreement and detail what the seller will be held accountable for in the event of an issue post-sale. They are specific and often cause heated debate between a buyer and a seller and between the lawyers. This is hard for an owner to pick up or even decide on, especially as they are personally involved in the warranty. An experienced advisor will have seen many legal documents and any consequences arising through warranties and is more likely to make an informed 'commercial' view and guide the owner without emotion, in addition to the lawyer's advice and counsel.

Business sale agreement/sale purchase agreement

The business sale agreement/contract is the legally binding agreement both parties will sign. The agreement must be drafted correctly to ensure you get paid and avoid disputes arising after you have sold your business.

A thorough sale agreement will include all the relevant information about the business pertaining to the sale and what is being acquired.

With the NBIO, you have a document that outlines and agrees on all relevant commercial terms without being legally binding. Based on this information, the business sale agreement/contract will be drawn up to become a legally binding agreement.

In addition to the general commercial and legal information, the contract should cover points such as:

- transfer of ownership of assets
- particular assets to be transferred
- confidentiality
- any condition precedent (CP)
- employees
- relevant warranties
- dispute resolution
- restraint clauses.

The key reason both parties should want an advisor leading the process on their behalf comes to keeping the whole process moving along and on track. It can be emotional, and several egos will be in play. An advisor really earns their money when, at the 11th hour, a 'deal breaker' issue has been discovered. They can keep a calm head and, as importantly, ensure that everyone else keeps theirs too. It also takes a certain discipline and experience to keep track of and keep discussions progressing when, typically, numerous issues need one or both of the lawyers' attention, and you are not their only client.

It is important to remember that at the point lawyers are introduced, a reasonable amount of time and effort has already been spent on the potential sale. The initial information would have been shared. There would have been many questions and meetings for the buyer to understand the business, the information provided, and the negotiations to produce an agreed NBIO. Emotionally, the buyer and seller have decided they want to do the deal and, subject to everything holding up in due diligence, believe they will complete it. It is, therefore, critical that while the legals must not be undermined and are very important, they must not be allowed to be deal stoppers. Without careful management, there is a potential risk they could.

Conditions Precedent (CP)

A buyer may like to check several areas of due diligence in detail. However, the owner may be nervous in case the deal doesn't go ahead, as they will need to provide access to critical areas of their business. To satisfy both parties' concerns, they may sign a binding agreement but with certain named Conditions Precedent (CP). This means that if one of the CPs is not satisfied, the buyer still has the right to some form of recourse, including pulling out of their binding offer (but only on the grounds of that particular CP). Common CPs include:

- key customers
- key suppliers

- key employees
- landlord reassigning a property lease.

Warranties

These are where the buyer, in effect, makes certain declarations about the business. Some buyers (and their lawyers) can be demanding in this area and request numerous onerous warranties. This can be one of the trickiest areas for negotiation in a sale agreement and one where an advisor can add value by ensuring that fair compromises are reached and discussions do not cease. An important point with warranties is that they are, in effect, holding the seller accountable for what happened in the business under their watch. If the seller has run a good business, hasn't broken any laws and has openly and fully disclosed everything in due diligence, they shouldn't have much to worry about. We encourage our clients to disclose everything in due diligence; then, the buyers have every chance to explore and discuss any potential issues.

Warranty insurance

This insurance protects the buyer in the event that the seller breaches the warranties and can be requested/forced to be paid for by the seller. It can be expensive and is another area where sensitive yet firm negotiations by the advisor on behalf of the buyer can be invaluable and save them a lot of money. *Note: Warranty insurance does not protect the seller or stop them from being liable for any claim.*

Conditions pre-completion

These are to cover 'normal behaviour' and can be quite detailed. Typically used when there is a time difference between signing a binding agreement and completion, and it isn't anything that should cause an issue.

Working capital/net tangible asset calculation

Part of the purchase price will involve the balance sheet/working capital/net tangible assets calculations. This can be a complicated set of calculations and requires qualified accountants to do the work and agree on both the methodology and the actual calculations. This can significantly affect the amount of money the seller receives for their business. As it is different for every situation and needs exact calculations, I am not going into any detail here. Still, please take warning: this is always an area of contention and upset that can be financially significant. I would strongly advise that very early in due diligence, both parties review a historical balance sheet and work through it together, line by line, to ensure everyone understands how it is likely to play out when it comes to completion and get it accurately documented for the lawyers to incorporate into the purchase agreement. The exact number will only be calculated with the completion balance sheet and is not usually known/calculated until three to four weeks post-completion (or even later in some cases).

CHAPTER 16

AFTER THE EVENT

Once the sale and purchase agreement has been signed, the purchase is legally binding and completion will follow (it is not always immediate). However, several completion and post-sale items need to occur, which can vary depending on the size and complexity of the business. These can include:

- delivery of certain documents by the seller
- paying taxes owed
- stocktake
- work-in-progress valuation
- completion statement
- assigning of property leases
- handing over of keys
- transferring of motor vehicles
- working capital calculation
- changing of bank account details
- changing of company name (sometimes)

- changeover of insurances
- external announcements, e.g. marketing
- novate agreements
- and many more!

In addition to the legal requirements post-sale, there are often commercial aspects to deal with. We discussed earlier that there might be an element of the purchase price linked with the future financial performance of the business, which can be over a couple of years. To maximise the total value of the deal, it is critical that the business owner is completely across the metrics of any performance-related payments, plays a key role in the delivery of any targets and is always updated with how the key performance indicators are tracked. It is usual that if there is a performance-based deferred element of a purchase, the owner is still in the business, playing a key role in the deferred aspects. If there is no requirement or desire for the owner to work in the business post-sale, I would strongly argue that there be no performance-related element.

It is worth spending the time and effort during the due diligence period and certainly before completion to fully detail the terms and conditions of any deferred, performance-based payment. For example, a common metric for deferred payment will be linked to the revenue from the clients a buyer is acquiring. This sounds simple enough, but what if one of those key clients stops transacting post-sale? Can the seller replace that client and associated revenue with a new client? Suppose the acquiring business does allow the seller to have a new client pipeline. In that case, it should be detailed by the individual businesses. Hence, it is clear that any revenue from that new client is included in the calculation for the deferred payment. I have seen too many ex-owners fall out with the acquirer and become disheartened in an earnout period. Putting aside any emotional aspects, the seller must have every opportunity to achieve their maximum earnout as it can be a significant part of the purchase price.

Variations of the deed

Sometimes, in an earnout situation, there can be sound reasons why it makes sense for one or both parties to renegotiate or reframe part or all of an earnout. For example, the buyer might want your services for another part of their business or want you to lead a special project and release you from the original earnout arrangements. However, they will need to allow you to earn the equivalent of your earnout in this case. A variation can sometimes be used to roll over a target for an extended period if there have been solid reasons why the original earnout was not achieved. Whatever the reason, any variation to the initial deed can only be with both parties' consent, and it will be a negotiation, just like the original sale of your business. Ensure you understand what is being requested or suggested and what you must do to achieve your earnout. I would also recommend it being written up and professionally executed by lawyers.

Deed of restraint

A deed of restraint is a very real and legally binding aspect of most sale transactions. Typically, a buyer will insist on a minimum restraint of trade of three years post-sale when the owner cannot work in the same industry as the business they just sold or compete in any way. This is a much stronger restraint than most owners are used to in employment contracts. The legal system will come down hard on someone who has significantly profited from the sale of their business and then actively competes against their old business.

SECTION 4

WHAT DO I DO NOW?

CHAPTER 17

DO I NEED AN ADVISOR?

In short, no, provided you have the knowledge and technical skills to complete a sale transaction. You would obviously still need to engage a lawyer and probably an accountant (for some parts). Still, I have tried to illustrate in this book that there are four principal reasons why you should invest in the best possible advisor you can.

1. **Selling a business is hard.** As I described earlier, in Australia, many businesses do not successfully complete a transaction (less than 1000 a year). You must do everything you can to maximise your chances of success.

2. **Time.** It takes an incredible amount of time and effort, not just the time spent in meetings but the research, finding buyers, pulling together the information required, responding to numerous questions, managing the legals, etc. You probably don't have that time, and it will take you longer than a professional. Also, even if you made the time, who runs your business while you disappear down a mine

shaft for six-plus months? You cannot afford your business's trading to slip during a sales process. Ideally, you would focus on driving revenue and profit growth.

3. **Maximising the sale value.** The price you get for your business is critical. An accomplished and successful advisor should be able to get you a significantly increased price for your business, provided you give them time and let them lead the process. Their fee becomes immaterial if the increase in additional value is many times repaid.

4. **Sanity.** Selling a business is usually emotional, even for the toughest business owners. In addition, the sales process is highly stressful and full of challenges and complications. What impact will that have on you, your family and your business if you go through the process alone?

What will it cost and is it worth it?

Advisors get paid for what they do for many reasons, most of which I hope you have understood from this book, but just a few things on their fee and fee structure. While advisor fees are wide-ranging, a good corporate advisor who does a significant amount of work (as opposed to a transaction-only organisation) will typically have two elements to their fee structure:

- **Retained fee.** As mentioned before, the amount of work, length of time and intensity of the engagement will dramatically affect the costs, and the retained monthly costs can vary significantly from $5K/month to $20K+/month.

- **Success fee.** This will also vary depending on the complication factor of your sale, the likelihood of success, the size of the business and the size of the retained fee. Still, you can expect a range of 3–10% of the total transaction price.

Ironically, you should be happy if your advisor gets a significant fee from selling your business because, providing the incentive was aligned correctly, they will have made you a lot more money than if you had saved their fee and done all the work yourself (possibly for a much lower price). To be happy to pay their fees, you must understand what they do and be satisfied that they will deliver an enhanced sale price for your business compared with if you did it yourself. If you do, you will see their fees as an investment. Just like any other investment you make in your business, you need to be satisfied that there is a compelling business case.

1. Retained fee

This can either be a monthly retainer or a fixed fee for specific 'chunks' of work. This can vary considerably, and three main elements will determine this cost:

1. **What they are attempting.** Are they simply preparing a business for sale? In this case, they are not being tasked with increasing the value of the business (apart from strong negotiating), so they will run their known process and engage the minimum staff required. In comparison, if they are working on a longer-term strategy of significantly increasing the value of the business, they will complete a strategic review, including analysing the industry you operate in, creating a growth plan, setting up a review process and running a program management function. It will be less predictable and more complicated, requiring different skills

and resources. Logically, the more complex option will have a higher cost (but should yield a much better sales price).

2. **How long they are engaged.** The complexity of the advisor's task will affect the length. Still, other factors include whether it is an international or a domestic sale, whether there are already known companies to target and how the market responds to a marketing campaign. Of course, the length of the sales process itself can vary significantly.

3. **The intensity of the engagement.** Assuming your advisor has unlimited resources and capability, they could engage more resources and assign them full-time to work on your business. While the short-term costs would be higher, the advisor could finish the work in less time than if they just worked on it, say, one day a week.

It is important to note that while the retained element of the fee may not be an insignificant sum, it will probably just cover the direct costs and recovery of overheads for the advisor. They will not make much profit out of their retainer fee. Therefore, it will not fully recompense them for their experience or added value to your business.

2. Success fee

This is payable only if a transaction is complete and where the advisor will make (and earn) their money. It is typically a percentage commission of the sale price. Still, as I have mentioned several times, selling a business is challenging. Hence, an advisor backs themselves to get your business sold and takes a significant financial risk if they don't. In short, their financial reward wholly aligns with your requirements, as does selling the business for the highest price. They will move heaven and earth to get both done for you. There is significant work an advisor does in a successful sales process that you won't ever see, including working weekends and many long days.

How do I find the right advisor (whom can I trust)?

Most good corporate advisors are well known and get regularly referred. As with many people we all work with in business, a referral or recommendation is a reliable and well-known method of selecting a new product or service supplier. But you should make an effort and do your due diligence on them and their business. For example, how many transactions have they personally completed, and I mean personally completed? While many large advisory companies will have bought and sold many companies, how many transactions has the senior partner completed? How much time will they personally be working on your sale, and how much will be done by a junior? This is important if you are selecting an organisation rather than an individual.

Once you are satisfied that they are competent and have enough experience, you must be sure you can trust them. While selling your business, you will have to disclose highly confidential (and sometimes personal) information, and there will be times when you don't see eye to eye with the advisor. Are they someone you could argue with, then forget it and move on five minutes later? I know this sounds a bit dramatic, but it is one of the most important business relationships you will ever have. You must be sure you can interact effectively with the person you select. It is similar to choosing a builder for an extensive rebuild of your house; you don't want to get halfway through the process and then decide to change builders. Many advisors work in their own way and have developed their methods through many transactions. If they have to pick up a client halfway through a process, they may want to start from the beginning and do their own analysis of your business.

Finally, are you happy that they represent you and your business? Their appearance, manner, style, attention to detail, work ethic, punctuality, proactiveness, etc., are all things that reflect on you. Your advisor will speak to a wide range of stakeholders for your business, including lawyers, future owners, customers, employees, suppliers, competitors, your bank, accountant and numerous other individuals and organisations. They will be the main point of contact for all communications with the future buyer. How they present themselves and respond to others will be a part of the buyer's evaluation when valuing your business and deciding whether to proceed with the sale.

Confidentiality

Regarding confidentiality, there are several aspects to consider. Most, if not all, advisors, brokers, agents or any other professional you engage when selling your business will keep all information and discussions confidential. Unless they are dishonest or have made a genuine mistake, your information will be safe with them. You should discuss with your advisor who else within your business and relevant business contacts will need to be engaged in the process and at what stage. You should have an open and frank discussion regarding your personal preference and the commercial risks associated with certain people knowing and at what stage. For example, most owners would ideally rather their employees or clients not know about a potential sale until a legally binding document is signed. However, this may not work for prospective buyers as they may want to engage with both key stakeholders as part of their due diligence. In this case, a compromise might be that neither is approached until an NBIO has been signed and, as part of due diligence, only a few in each category know the process (for example, the top five clients and only key staff). Alternatively, a common practice is to split the signing of a binding agreement and completion and have a CP. The timing of who knows what, when and how they are communicated with should form a key part of the transition plan, which commences well before completion.

As for any external parties (prospective buyers) who get access to your information, they will have to sign a confidentiality agreement. If the sale does not go through with them, they need to actively destroy all information provided to them.

What are the golden rules of working with an advisor?

Once you have determined the type and cost of your advisor, hopefully, you will have picked one you can trust. You should agree on a clear timetable of likely meetings, events and work schedules so you are comfortable that they are doing what they said they would. Like any external professional, they will do most of their work outside of your offices, so you need a process to know where things are up to. A good advisor will present a work plan and ask for your sign-off.

Secondly, you must let them do what you are paying them for. There is no point in engaging a top advisor if you then decide to engage directly with the potential acquirer. Sure, you will need to build a relationship with the new owner, but allow the advisor to lead the process. They will know what meetings you should be in and what level of engagement you need to have.

Finally, trust them. Sometimes, they will provide advice that is different from what you would have done. By all means, have a robust discussion and make your views clear. You will always have the ultimate authority over any decision, but remember why you engaged them. They will have been through each step many times before, particularly negotiation tactics (including turning down offers). You have to trust their judgement; otherwise, you might as well have just engaged a cheaper resource to assist you with only the technical aspects of the transaction.

CHAPTER 18

NEXT STEPS

Go for a walk. Leave your phone behind and think through if you are ready to sell your business. Discuss it with your partner. Ask yourself what you will do after the sale:

Will you retire?

Will you continue to work in the business but report to the new owner's structure?

Will you travel?

Will you want to set up another business again at some point?

While I am not encouraging you to procrastinate, selling a business is one of the most significant life events a person can have, and you must be sure about it. At the same time, do not worry about the how; there are good people who can help you.

Once you have made up your mind, do it! You cannot start early enough.

While writing this book, I have reflected on what I believe are the key ingredients to maximising value and successfully selling. While everything is important, I believe there are three things you have to do to give yourself the very best chance of maxing out and achieving the best value you can get for your business.

1. Take the time

As I have said throughout this book, to maximise the value of your business and achieve the best sales price, you need time to build and realise the value within your business. You must allow yourself and your advisor at least nine months before actively putting it on the market (ideally longer). It is evident that if you want to demonstrate long-lasting value to a prospective buyer, that value has to be authentic. You must have properly evaluated your business, built a long-term strategic plan and executed it (or at least part of it). You can't just say a business has value by hiring a clever writer/presenter. For someone to pay significant money, you must demonstrate that its value is real, especially if you want recognition in the offer price for the business's future value.

But don't take too long

I am not contradicting myself here. I know I have said to take your time, but I didn't say it was acceptable or value-adding to waste it or procrastinate! Remember, taking too long once you are in a sales process with a potential buyer is one of the ways a deal can get killed. You must make progress every day (and your business needs to perform at its best while this is happening).

If you ignore everything else in this book, please do not underestimate or undervalue the importance of time, in fully preparing a business before a sale and being effective and proactive (with time) when engaged with a buyer.

2. Hire the best

Why would you hire the lowest-skill resource to maximise the value of your business in a sales process? If you believe what I have described in this book, then unless you have all the skills and experience and can altogether remove yourself from the business for 12 months without negatively affecting its revenue or profit, you need to engage a professional. If by hiring the best resource you can, they double the amount you would have received for your business, why wouldn't you do it and pay the associated fees to achieve it?

Find the organisation, and more importantly, find the individual you believe can do this for you and with whom you feel comfortable. Engage them to deliver what you require and what your business deserves. It is not easy, even with the best advisor. Still, if you have a strong advisor with a trusted and proven process and you are determined, you will be amazed at how much you can achieve. You have run a successful business for many years. You owe it to yourself, your family, employees, clients and suppliers to ensure that your last action in your business is a success.

3. Establish credibility

People buy from people. You know this as while your business may have fantastic products or services, what keeps clients coming back is you and your staff. A sale of a business is no different.

Of course, the key metrics of the business have to be right, as do the prospects for your business. While it may not stop a deal from going ahead, if you or your advisor have not built up strong credibility with an acquirer, they will not pay their maximum and may decide not to proceed. Every interaction, phone call and document will form part of their view of you and your business. If an owner's or advisor's credibility is lost with a buyer, it is almost impossible to get it back.

CONCLUSION

This book is all about how to maximise the value of your business. The title states you can achieve a $30M price for your business. This may not be the case; it could be worth more or less. However, I have tried to illustrate that in every business, there is a risk that significant hidden value is not realised. When a business owner sells, they can leave considerable wealth for the next person. My aim in life is to ensure that the current business owner should be the one to realise the maximum value possible for their business. But there is an added and sometimes hidden complexity to achieving the maximum sale price that may not at first glance be obvious. I have detailed in the book the six-step process I follow to deliver value and achieve a successful sale; others may have a similar approach. However, there is much more to this than just a process; otherwise, surely lots of advisors, accountants, brokers, etc., would be offering to do what I have detailed. In addition to having a great process, the advisor needs the right blend of skills, experience and personal attributes.

Your advisor must have been on a particular journey themselves to have gained the knowledge, experience (including their fair share of mistakes) and successes to deliver all aspects to execute everything I have detailed. Many organisations and individuals can provide some of what is required, but very few can do it all. An advisor needs the following to be able to deliver the entire program:

- Many years of experience in starting, running and even closing down businesses.
- Experience in building and executing long-term strategies for complicated businesses.
- Solid financial understanding and capability.
- Significant program management experience.
- Strong people skills.
- Several successful business sale transactions, including a significant number as a buyer.
- Significant negotiating experience and skill.
- An understanding of the legal process and experience in negotiating many sale and purchase agreements.

It is not enough to have a great process, though you certainly must have one. You need to engage a person/business with all the necessary attributes and experience to deliver such a program. There is no reason why you cannot achieve life-changing wealth and free yourself from the shackles of running a business every day.

This book was not written to include every exact detail, process or item to be considered when selling a business. I may have over-emphasised some aspects of the process and not gone into enough detail on others or even covered them at all. It was written to give the reader a deeper insight into the process and, more importantly, some of the key areas that a business owner needs to consider to maximise the value of their business when selling. Please take qualified advice regarding your specific circumstances to ensure that your needs and nuances are well covered.

I hope you have enjoyed reading this book and are inspired to start. If you would like to know more about anything I have covered, please do not hesitate to contact me or my business. We would love to hear from you.

'Start where you are.
Use what you have.
Do what you can.'

Arthur Ashe

GLOSSARY OF TERMS

adjusted or normalised EBITDA – Removal of non-recurring expenses or revenue from EBITDA to project the future earnings a prospective buyer might expect.

assets – Items within the company of value that can be turned into cash (Note: cash itself is an asset).

capital expenditure (CapEx) – Funds spent by a company to acquire, upgrade or maintain physical assets, such as property, equipment or infrastructure.

condition precedent (CP) – Items that are not disclosed in the usual due diligence process but need to be completed before completion. These items are only disclosed once a prospective buyer has confirmed (and is legally bound to acquire the business apart from any issues with a particular CP item) that it has successfully completed due diligence on all other items.

data room – A secure online platform for storing, organising and sharing confidential documents and information during business transactions.

deferred consideration – The consideration payable after completion, not subject to variation depending on the performance of the business, securities or assets.

discounted cash flow (DCF) – A valuation method used to estimate the attractiveness of an investment opportunity. It takes future free cash flow projections and discounts them to estimate the current value.

earnout consideration – The consideration payable after completion, subject to the performance of the business, assets and/or securities.

EBITDA – Earnings (net income) before interest, tax, depreciation or amortisation.

gross margin – The difference between revenue and cost of goods sold, divided by revenue expressed as a percentage. Generally, it is calculated as the selling price of an item, less the cost of goods sold, then divided by the same selling price.

gross profit – The profit a company makes after deducting those costs and expenses it directly incurs producing and selling its goods or services.

initial information – Initial information required for a prospective buyer to value a business and submit an NBIO.

initial public offering (IPO) – The process by which a privately-held company offers shares of its stock to the public for the first time to be traded on the stock exchange.

intellectual property (IP) – legally protected creations, such as inventions, trademarks and trade secrets, fostering innovation and granting exclusive rights to creators for commercial benefits.

liabilities – Obligations of the company. They are amounts owed by the company to all creditors.

net profit – The profit a company makes after deducting all costs that were not deducted when producing the gross profit figure. It is the actual/real profit of a business.

net assets – The value of a company's assets minus its liabilities. ((total fixed assets + total current assets) – (total current liabilities + total long-term liabilities)).

non-binding indicative offer (NBIO) – A short-form document detailing the material commercial terms of a potential deal. It is not legally binding but establishes a contractual negotiating framework between potential buyer and seller as they work towards a definitive sale and purchase agreement. Also known as a *letter of intent (LOI)*.

private equity (PE) – Invest in private companies or acquire their ownership stakes, aiming to enhance value, restructure operations, and eventually sell for profit, often within a defined period.

revenue – The income a business receives from its normal business activities. Also known as *sales* or *turnover*.

return on investment (ROI) – A ratio between net income and investment. Also known as *return on costs*.

sale purchase agreement (SPA) – A legal agreement between a seller and purchaser detailing what is and isn't included in the sale of a business. It goes beyond just the price and includes the various terms and conditions associated with the sale.

work-in-progress – The monetary value of goods and services that have not yet been completed.

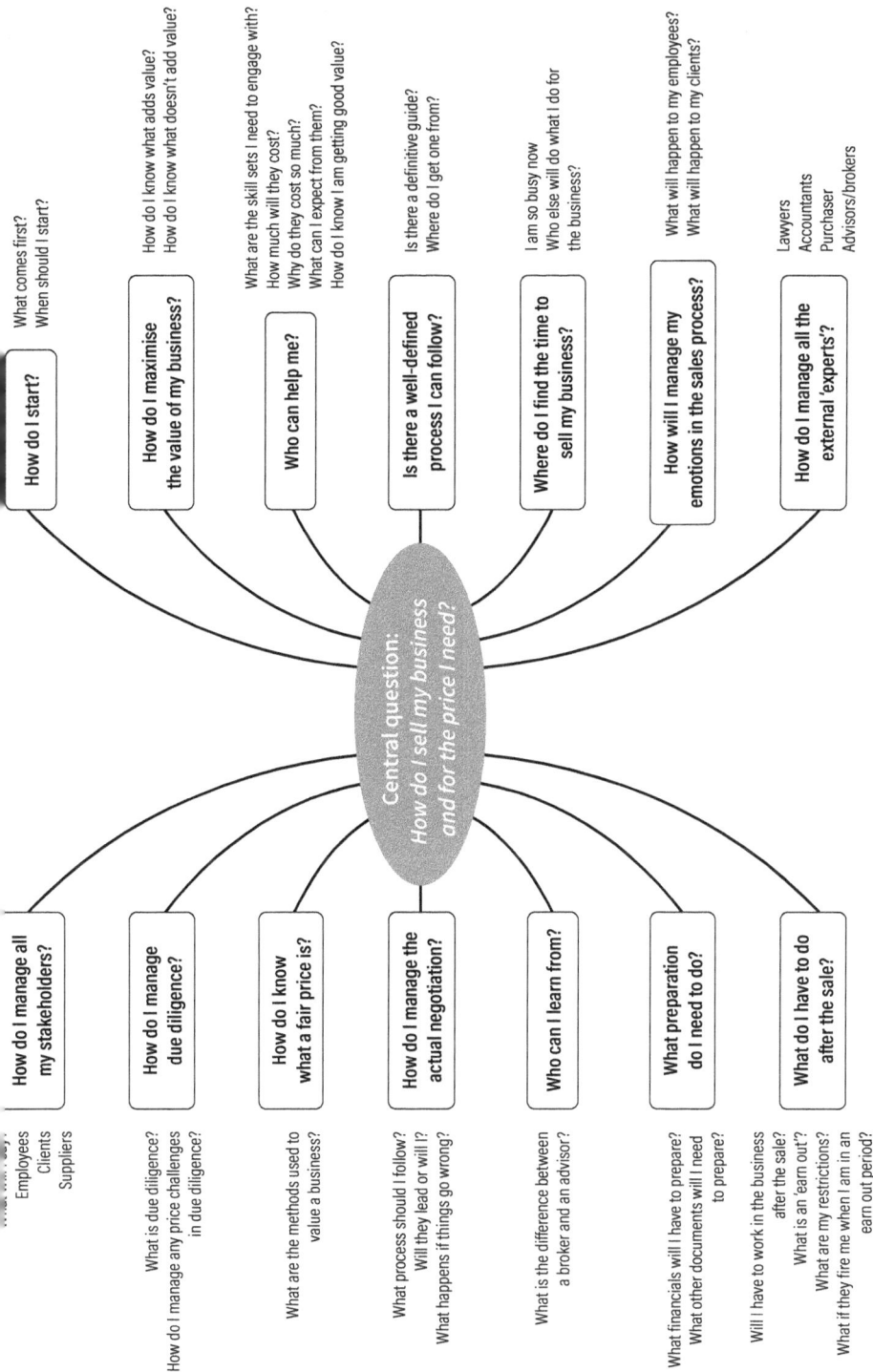

Central question: How do I sell my business and for the price I need?

How do I start?
- What comes first?
- When should I start?

How do I maximise the value of my business?
- How do I know what adds value?
- How do I know what doesn't add value?

Who can help me?
- What are the skill sets I need to engage with?
- How much will they cost?
- Why do they cost so much?
- What can I expect from them?
- How do I know I am getting good value?

Is there a well-defined process I can follow?
- Is there a definitive guide?
- Where do I get one from?

Where do I find the time to sell my business?
- I am so busy now
- Who else will do what I do for the business?

How will I manage my emotions in the sales process?

How do I manage all the external 'experts'?
- What will happen to my employees?
- What will happen to my clients?
- Lawyers
- Accountants
- Purchaser
- Advisors/brokers

How do I manage all my stakeholders?
- Employees
- Clients
- Suppliers

How do I manage due diligence?
- What is due diligence?
- How do I manage any price challenges in due diligence?

How do I know what a fair price is?
- What are the methods used to value a business?

How do I manage the actual negotiation?
- What process should I follow?
- Will they lead or will I?
- What happens if things go wrong?

Who can I learn from?
- What is the difference between a broker and an advisor?

What preparation do I need to do?
- What financials will I have to prepare?
- What other documents will I need to prepare?

What do I have to do after the sale?
- Will I have to work in the business after the sale?
- What is an 'earn out'?
- What are my restrictions?
- What if they fire me when I am in an earn out period?

www.ingramcontent.com/pod-product-compliance
Lightning Source LLC
Chambersburg PA
CBHW040858210326
41597CB00029B/4888